Research on Whole Language

Support for a New Curriculum

Diane Stephens

University of Illinois
at Urbana-Champaign

Richard C. Owen Publishers, Inc., Katonah, New York

Library of Congress Catalog Card Number:

91-067299

ISBN: 1-878450-13-1

Richard C. Owen Publishers, Inc.
135 Katonah Avenue
Katonah, New York 10536

Printed in the United States of America.

9 8 7 6 5 4 3 2 1

Contents

Preface   v

Part I   Whole Language in Historical Perspective   1

Part II   Whole Language as Philosophy   5

          The "Whole" in Whole Language   6
          What We Know About Learning Outside
              of School   7
          Teachers as Informed Professionals   9
          Teachers as Empowered Professionals   11

Part III Whole Language as Practice   13

          Understanding Learning in Whole Language
              Classrooms   17
          Comparing Learning   17
          Understanding Teaching   19
          Directions for Future Research   20
          Annotated Bibliography   23

References   59

Preface

Two years ago, people started writing and calling—asking me for the bibliography of whole language research on which they had heard I had been working. At first, I simply informed them that I was not working on a bibliography. Eventually, I decided that I might as well meet the demand. After all, what could be so hard? I would just pull together the research, annotate it, and meet a need that many seemed to have.

Things were not as simple as I had imagined them to be, and it soon became apparent that many questions needed to be addressed before I could "just pull together the research." What, for example, was "whole language"? What was "research"? And, even if I had definitions for each, how would I decide if a particular article or a report was "whole language" or "research"? Did I want to annotate the research that formed the foundation *for* a whole language philosophy (the work of linguists, sociolinguists, philosophers, psychologists, and sociologists, for example), or did I want research *on* whole language (the practices of teachers who held a whole language philosophy)? Did I even want to call the document a "whole language" bibliography? Was there a better, less controversial, label?

After a year or so, I pretty much had these issues worked out; I had definitions and categories for inclusion and exclusion (see Parts II and III for an explanation of these criteria); I had decided to use the "whole language" label. I also had located, read, and annotated most of the studies that are included here. I then sat down to write a "short introduction" to the annotations. Pleased to be done with the bibliography, I asked friends and colleagues to respond to the document.

In *Love You Forever*, Robert Munsch tells of a child: "He grew and he grew and he grew. He grew until he was. . . ." That line echoes in my mind as I sit to write this (last?) version of my "short introduction." Each person who read the original introduction made both general and specific suggestions for revision *and* suggested that I add more—more about whole language itself, more about the politics of whole language, and more about the relationship between oral and written language. The introduction grew and grew and grew.

I shared the revised text with the individuals who had made the original suggestions, as well as with educators and parents encountering the text for the first time. The response was familiar: general and specific suggestions and requests for more—more about why I chose the studies, more about whole language as a label, more about the disciplines that contributed to a whole language philosophy. The introduction grew and grew and grew. I began to find humor in possible titles (e.g., *Whole Language: Annotated Studies, with a Very Long Introduction*).

Still the introduction grew and grew and grew. Judith Newman, a close friend who thoughtfully read many versions, wondered if I wasn't trying to make the text all things to all people and worried about the accommodations I was making in order to please multiple audiences. Richard Owen rather tactfully suggested that I make it clear just what the introduction was about. It had grown and grown and grown, and even I wasn't sure what it had become. What was I trying to do? Did I need all the parts I had written? Would it be best to return to a simple, short preface to the annotations?

In the end, I decided to reorganize the text into three major sections. My original intent simply had been to pull together the research on whole language. However, with each study I gathered and annotated, and with each request I received for the work in progress, I became more and more aware of the debate over whole language and of how the field was polarized by the debate. I grew increasingly concerned that we were putting our

vi

energies into responding to each other instead of into helping children. I began to think that, if we could share an understanding about whole language (instead of fight over what *it* was), we might see that our similarities outweighed our differences. From a common ground, we might be able to work with, not against, each other. Together we might make a difference in the lives of children. From that perspective, the research I was annotating (Part III) simply became one means of understanding whole language. Putting the label in historical perspective (Part I) and discussing the philosophy (Part II) seemed to be two other contributions I could make to developing a shared understanding about whole language.

Whole language and research on whole language are both clearly in their beginning stages. The label was virtually unknown twenty years ago. (See Yetta Goodman, 1989, for a history of the concept.) Thirty-one of the thirty-eight studies cited here have been conducted since 1985; only one was published before 1980. Some wager that it is a field that will never see adulthood. They argue that whole language will simply die out or that the ideas represented within a whole language philosophy will be subsumed under similar ideas from other fields: hands-on science, community-based social studies, authentic problem solving in mathematics. Others see whole language as broadening, not only to accompany and to represent the demand for authentic education within content areas, but also to encompass the cries for teacher empowerment, reflective practitioners, school-based management, and curricular alternatives that support the learning of children from diverse cultures. Woven into the debates are arguments about "whole language" as a label.

However, neither the longevity nor the advisability of the label is at issue here. Indeed, issues of longevity and of label, like those of personality and rhetorical style, have made it difficult for participants in the debate to even hear, let alone understand, one another. Rather, the question being addressed is simply this: What is whole language? I hope this text begins to answer this question, that it meets the needs of those who have called and have written, and that it helps move the field from debate to dialogue. Perhaps, more importantly, I hope it helps those who teach and those who learn. I hope that it helps with Monday morning.

Part I

Whole Language in Historical Perspective

For many years, reading educators have debated about how best to teach reading. (For an excellent discussion of early reading education, see Nila Banton Smith's *American Reading Education,* 1988.) On one side, there are those who believe that reading should be "whole word" or "look-say," and, on the other side, there are those who believe that children first need to learn the letters of the alphabet and the sounds that those letters make. The debates have gone back and forth over a number of decades. Some educators have argued that research proves the superiority of one method over another; others have contested those results. (For a 1990's version of this debate, see *Education Week,* March 28, 1990, and *The Reading Teacher,* February and March 1990). Meanwhile, the methods themselves have ebbed and waned in popularity.

In the 1960's, the content and tenor of the debate began to change. A new branch of psychology, cognitive psychology, offered theories of comprehension. Some linguists turned their attention to how language was learned. An even newer field, psycholinguistics, emerged. Other linguists began to study language in use and called themselves sociolinguists. In this process, literacy education was redefined. Questions of pedagogy became embedded in multiple knowledge bases about language learning. The very questions that were asked reflected the way educators viewed reading and writing. Sociolinguists, for example, asked about the social and cultural cues from which children learned to "do school," and psycholinguists asked how children learned words and concepts and how they acquired complex cognitive constructs. Rather than a separate field, literacy instruction became the domain of many fields.

The labeling of disciplines and debates over pedagogy, most of which was occurring at the university level, grew increasingly complex. In the midst of this complexity, some educators, informed by the debate, began to label themselves. Some aligned themselves with "process writing"; others, with "literature-based instruction." Still others called themselves "whole language" teachers. Sometimes as participants in college classes and sometimes independent of university influence, these teachers

2

read what was being written, talked with each other about class-room implications, and developed what Kathy Short (1985) calls "practiceable theory"—ways of moving research and theory into practice. As they experimented and tried out classroom techniques, these teachers began developing a sense of what did and did not work in their classrooms. They shared these practices with each other informally and occasionally formed networks and held meetings within their community. Eventually, some groups scheduled statewide and national meetings. For example, Teachers Applying Whole Language (TAWL) groups meet at the annual conventions of the International Reading Association (IRA) and the National Council of Teachers of English (NCTE). In 1989, TAWL groups formed their own national organization, the Whole Language Umbrella, which held its first national con-ference in St. Louis in August 1990.

Teachers also wrote about what they were learning. Arti-cles appeared in *Language Arts, The Reading Teacher, Teaching K-8,* and *Teachers Networking,* as well as in many state and local publications. Teacher-authored chapters and books began to ap-pear, for example, *In the Middle* (Atwell, 1987); *Portraits of Whole Language Classrooms* (Mills and Clyde, 1990); *Breaking Ground: Teachers Relate Reading and Writing in the Elementary School* (Newkirk and Atwell, 1984); *Whole Language: Theory in Use* (Newman, 1985); *Finding Our Own Way* (Newman, 1990); *Transi-tions* (Routman, 1989); *What Matters: A Primer for Teaching Read-ing* (Stephens, 1990).

In their writing and in their dialogues, teachers from public schools and universities began to make explicit the understand-ings they shared among themselves and with other educators; they also began to identify differences. Ultimately, and perhaps unfortunately, some ideas—"whole language," for example— became reified. Perhaps curious about this "new" thing, other educators asked what whole language was, what *it* looked like, and whether or not *it* worked. Some wanted "whole language" defined so that it could be more easily shared, studied, or imple-mented. Others argued that "whole language" was not an object or a thing—a something that could be defined; rather, they

3

claimed, "whole language" was a set of ideas, a way of thinking, and an approach to schooling, teaching, and learning. Those who conceptualized "whole language" as a thing became frustrated by the lack of definition. Those who conceptualized "whole language" as a way of thinking became frustrated by the requests for a definition.

Dialogue, discussion, and debate, made possible only by a common knowledge base, became difficult, even impossible without shared understandings. Unable reasonably to consider differences of substance, educators began arguing about differences of style and of personality. Somewhere along the way, they even seemed to forget that they were united by their concern for the education of children.

Part II

Whole Language
as Philosophy

W hen I first became aware of how children learn to talk, I was struck by the "wholeness" of the experience. Parents and other talkers do not separate language into parts and then teach the child, part by part, sound by sound. Rather, people use "whole" language to talk to, and with, children. Children, surrounded by the language and understanding its functions (Halliday, 1975), want to participate in the discourse. They do so by inferring the rules of language and trying them out (Bowerman, 1982; Brown, 1970; Read, 1975). The "wholeness" of oral language learning includes the language itself, the function it serves, and the context within which it occurs. Oral language learning thus reveals itself as a social and a historical process. A history of shared experiences, for example, makes it easier to understand the meaning of the toddler's language.

The "Whole" in Whole Language

When this "whole" language perspective is applied to written language learning, similar patterns emerge. It becomes apparent that written language learning, like oral language learning, is a social, historical process that involves language, function, and context. "Whole" language reveals itself as one means for knowing our world and as the dominant means through which we share and reflect upon what it is we know. Because we use language both to know and to change our world, language is political. It offers opportunity for power and control. Degree of access to language, whether oral or written, influences the functions that language serves. To constrain access is to limit knowing. Reading *only* fiction or *only* non-fiction, *only* worksheet pages or *only* directions written on the board, constrains what children can learn. Teachers are similarly constrained if they read *only* about theory or *only* about practice or *only* the directions in the teacher's manual.

A whole language perspective, then, is more than an emphasis on "whole" books or on functional uses of "whole" texts.

Whole language is a way of thinking about teaching and learning and of the role of language in those contexts. As such, whole language is an ever evolving agenda. As we enter the 1990's, the following beliefs drive that agenda:

1. Learning in school ought to incorporate what is known about learning outside of school.

2. Teachers should base curricular decisions on what is known about language and learning, should possess and be driven by a vision of literacy, should use observation to inform teaching, and should reflect continuously.

3. Teachers as professionals are entitled to a political context that empowers them as informed decision makers.

What We Know About Learning Outside of School

Research from many disciplines has contributed to the knowledge base about literacy. From sociology, we have learned about cultural differences and how they impact on school. We know that misunderstandings can result when homogeneity is expected from a heterogeneous population (Heath, 1983; Delpit, 1988; García, Jiménez, and Pearson, 1989). From cognitive psychology, we have discovered that individuals can only learn about those things about which they already possess some knowledge (Anderson, Spiro, and Anderson, 1978; Pearson, Hansen, and Gordon, 1979; Rumelhart and Ortony, 1977). We also know that learning involves both self-awareness and self-monitoring (Baker and Brown, 1984; Brown, 1980; Brown, Campione, and Day, 1981; Flavell, 1976). From research on critical thinking, we found that learning is a meaning-making process that involves making, testing, and revising hypotheses (Cornbleth, 1987; Neisser, 1976; Neilsen, 1989; Siegel and Carey, 1989). From scholars in the fields of sociolinguistics, anthropology, and critical theory we have come to understand the

7

importance of situating language within social, cultural, and historical contexts (Apple, 1983; Bloome and Green, 1984; Everhart, 1983; Fraatz, 1987; Giroux, 1984; Popkewitz, 1987). They have helped us understand school literacy as a socially constructed event.

Extensive studies of out-of-school language learning have confirmed that language learning is both a social and a cultural process. One cannot learn language unless one interacts with already proficient language users (Vygotsky, 1962). What one learns is highly influenced by the cultural norms and expectations of one's culture (Heath, 1983; Ogbu, 1986). We also know that language learning is a rule-making process. Children imitate neither written nor oral language; rather, they infer the rules and then try them out (Brown, 1970; Read, 1975). This explains children's use of language they have never heard ("I gots two feets") or seen ("I! am! 8! today!").

Children acquire knowledge about both written and oral language before they come to school (Baghban, 1984; Bissex, 1980; Ferreiro and Teberosky, 1979; Harste, Woodward, and Burke, 1984; Holdaway, 1979, 1986; Jaggar and Smith-Burke, 1985; Sulzby and Teale, 1987; Taylor, 1983). This knowledge comes from children's active engagement with language. Children learn about oral language because they are surrounded by it and because they actively participate in discourse (Brown, 1970; Carey, 1982; Clark, 1977, 1978; Halliday, 1975, 1982; Lindfors, 1985; Wells, 1986). So, too, do children learn written language (Clay, 1972; Durkin, 1966; Goodman, 1984; Graves, 1983; Hansen, 1987; Newman, 1984; Purcell-Gates, 1988; Sampson, 1986; Teale and Martinez, 1987).

Because of variability in these engagements, some children come to school with a great deal of knowledge about both oral and written language, while others come with considerably less. Those who come to school with more knowledge have a greater chance of succeeding in school than those who come with less (Johnston and Allington, in press; Stanovich, 1986; Wells, 1986). A variety of preschool, remedial, intervention, and special education programs have been designed to address this inequity.

Reading Recovery (Clay, 1972), for example, is currently used in several cities in the United States, as well as in New Zealand and Australia, in an attempt to accelerate the reading progress of first-grade children "at-risk" for school failure.

What we know is extensive, critical, and useful. Indeed, within the field of reading education there has been nearly unanimous agreement with Richard Anderson et al.'s introduction to *Becoming a Nation of Readers* (1985): "The knowledge is now available to make worthwhile improvements in reading throughout the United States. If the practices seen in the classrooms of the best teachers in the best schools could be introduced everywhere, the improvements in reading would be dramatic."

Teachers as Informed Professionals

Much of what we currently know about language and learning is relatively new. Most of the information simply did not exist twenty years ago. As new information has been acquired, it has been shared both formally and informally through conversations, conferences, classes, inservice programs, newspapers, journal articles, and books. However, keeping current is a time-consuming task. In addition, the sharing is not evenly distributed; some professors and teachers have more access to information than others. As a result, just as with language learners, there are some educators who come to the classroom knowing more and some who come knowing less.

How can this inequity be best addressed? Some educators believe that, because building a broad knowledge base is difficult and time consuming, it is necessary to develop shortcuts. One shortcut is to simplify or to reduce the information into "practicable" form. For example, a great deal is known about learning as a social process. As a means of using some of this knowledge base to improve instruction, short inservice training sessions are sometimes scheduled on cooperative learning (Johnson and Johnson, 1979; Slavin, 1983). These training sessions outline a prescriptive structure for teaching. Because the training focuses on method rather than philosophy, participants are able to *do* cooperative learning without understanding the knowledge base upon which it is built. This means that cooperative learning can be a part of classroom instruction without really affecting classroom contexts. (As one teacher noted, "We have Cooperative Learning on Friday at 1:00.") Similarly, without access to the corresponding knowledge bases, it is possible to *do* critical thinking without helping students think critically; *do* literature-based reading instruction without enhancing the students' abilities either to read or to understand literature; *do* process writing without developing writing fluency; and *do* whole language without supporting language growth.

Other educators believe that simply asking, telling, or training teachers to *do* is problematic. Concerned with the politics of control and particularly sensitive to the sometimes inadvertent use of knowledge to control, these educators argue that teaching, schooling, and learning can only improve if teachers have *direct* access to the research base (Apple, 1983; Edelsky, 1988; Shannon, 1989a, 1989b; Simon, 1987; Watson, Burke, and Harste, 1988). They also argue that teachers should be contributors to the knowledge base. Whole language educators, focusing on the contexts and uses of literacy, share this view.

There are, of course, various avenues for teachers to gain access to, and be contributors to, what is known. New books, journal articles, pamphlets, and newsletters written by university and public school educators report, summarize, or synthesize research (see Avery, 1985; Boutwell, 1983; Church and Newman, 1985; Five, 1985; and McConaghy, 1986 for examples of contributions by public school educators). Self-study groups meet to share observations and to discuss readings. Public school and university educators have collaborated on research (see Allen and Carr, 1989; Allen et al., 1989; Clyde, 1987; Cousins, 1988; Edelsky, Draper, and Smith, 1983; Hanssen, in process; Michalove, 1989; Pierce, 1984; Short, 1985; Stephens, 1986). Some public schools have arranged long-term consultation arrangements with university educators who have various areas of expertise (Clarke, 1987). Still other schools have worked collaboratively with local universities in long-term projects designed to develop the knowledge base of both public school and university faculties (Florio-Ruane, 1986; García et al., 1989).

Many of these attempts to acknowledge teacher contributions to the knowledge base and to give them direct access to the knowledge base developed by others are very recent, and we are just beginning to be able to look across projects to identify patterns. Preliminary findings, however, suggest that, when public school teachers have access to, and are creators of, the knowledge base, when they know about language, learning, teaching, and children, they make informed curricular decisions that support the learning of their students (Stephens, 1988).

Teachers as Empowered Professionals

In a recent study, David Wendler, S. Jay Samuels, and Vienna K. Moore (1989) looked at the reading instruction of various groups of teachers—award-winning teachers, teachers with masters' degrees, and a control group. The results of this study suggest that there were no significant differences in the reading instruction provided by the three different groups of teachers. In the thirty-six classrooms studied, the knowledge that Richard Anderson et al. (1985) talked about was not being incorporated into instruction. Reading instruction was not approached as if reading were the social, interpretative, meaning-making process we know it to be.

This study would suggest that neither being a "good" teacher nor taking master's level classes in reading guarantees qualitatively different comprehension instruction. However, David Wendler, S. Jay Samuels, and Vienna K. Moore (1989) do not tell us about the knowledge base of the teachers. We do not know whether the teachers *had* a broad knowledge base about literacy instruction. It is possible that they did not. Perhaps, more importantly, we also do not know if the political context of the schools allowed teachers to use their knowledge base to inform decision making at the classroom, building, and district levels. All too often, observational studies of classrooms suggest that schools are set up so that curriculum is driven by materials and mandates, rather than by informed reflection (Durkin, 1978–1979; Harste and Stephens, 1985; Stephens et al. 1990). One teacher, for example, was told that she could not share with parents the success of the reading and writing workshop she had established for her inner-city fifth- and sixth-grade students. The school board had decided what books were to be used to teach reading and writing, and to publicize that a teacher had deviated from the board mandate would put both the teacher's and the principal's jobs at risk—in spite of the overwhelming success of the program. In addition, she was told she would have to stop teaching reading and writing and, instead, teach for the reading and writing test (Story, 1988).

Unfortunately, literacy instruction has become almost synonymous with covering a set of externally mandated objectives or a series of basal readers. From the perspective of many in the field, including whole language educators, teachers need to be able to use their knowledge to inform their decision making. Our schools and our school children can no longer afford to have critical curricular and instructional decisions made outside the classrooms. Teachers, as professionals, need an extensive knowledge base from which to make decisions, and they need contexts that enable them to act on those decisions.

Part III

Whole Language
as Practice

L anguage creates illusions. The words we use cause us to think we agree, when, in practice, we find we do not. The reverse is also true: We think we disagree when, in practice, only our labels are different. This text contains annotations of research on whole language practice in the hope that descriptions will enable us to move past illusion and debate to understanding. The case studies help us to see the individual student, ostensibly the ultimate benefactor of all educational efforts. Descriptive classroom research allows us to revisit the classroom through the eyes of the writer. Comparative studies help us to understand one way of "doing school" by juxtaposing it with another.

In order to locate these kinds of studies, I searched several on-line databases, explored dissertation abstracts, and skimmed the tables of contents of all major literacy journals from 1974 to 1989. I sent for papers presented at national conferences. I shared my working drafts with whole language educators, asking them to check my bibliography against their knowledge base, so as to identify studies I might have overlooked.

Once a study had been located, I read the entire document and included it if (1) the study represented scholarly reflection rather than an anecdotal recollection of events and (2) the classroom descriptions or instructional programs were consistent with whole language as philosophy. I considered the following characteristics as consistent with a whole language philosophy:

1. Children were engaged as learners. They used language to make and test hypotheses, to explore possibilities, to reflect on what they had learned, and to decide about what they wanted to learn next.

2. Teachers were engaged as learners. They saw themselves as professionals, read widely, and reflected often. They planned extensively, revised as necessary, and assessed continuously. Their observations, reflections, and decision making were driven by their vision of what it meant to be literate and educated. They established

14

environments that facilitated learning and used demonstration and response as primary teaching tools.

3. Learning was a social process, and transactions among
   teachers, students, and curriculum significantly contributed to the learning that had occurred.

4. Texts in use were whole, cohesive documents that
   served a purpose for the learner and had an audience
   broader than just the teacher.

I then divided the studies into two categories: case studies
of individual children, and descriptive and comparative classroom studies. The length of annotation of each study was related
to the amount of information it provided (a five-page journal
article versus a five hundred-page research report), as well as to
the ease of availability of the research report. For example, many
times only parts of qualitative studies are reported in journal
articles. The "thick description" of classroom events, essential to
understanding whole language as practice, often are captured
only in the original research report, many of which are disserta-
tions or master's degree theses and thus difficult to obtain. I
decided to provide enough information about these harder-to-
obtain texts so that readers could determine which documents
they wanted to peruse in their entirety.

Figure 1. Studies by Researcher(s)

Researchers	Publication Date	Grade Level	Comparative Study?[1]	Includes At-Risk Population?[2]
Allen	1988	K	No	Yes
Allen & Carr	1989	K	No	Yes
Allen, Michalove, West, & Shockley	1989	1,2	No	Yes
Avery	1985	1	No	No
Barone & Lovell	1987	2	No	No
Boutwell	1983	3	No	No
Brabson	in process	Special Education	No	Yes

15

Figure 1. Studies by Researcher(s) *(continued)*

Researchers	Publication Date	Grade Level	Comparative Study?[1]	Includes At-Risk Population?[2]
Church & Newman	1985	9	No	Yes
Clyde	1987	Preschool	No	No
Cousins	1988	Special Education	No	Yes
Crowley	in process	1,2,3,4,5	No	No
Dahl & Freppon	in process	K,1	Yes	Yes
DeFord	1981	1	Yes	No
DeLawter	1975	1	Yes	No
Dobson	1988	K,1	Yes	Yes
Edelsky, Draper, & Smith	1983	6	No	Yes
Five	1985	5	No	Yes
Freppon	1988	1	Yes	No
Gunderson & Shapiro	1987	1	Yes	No
Gunderson & Shapiro	1988	1	No	No
Hagerty, Hiebert, & Owens	1989	2,4,6	Yes	No
Hanssen	in process	8	No	No
Haussler	1982	K,1	No	No
McConaghy	1986	1	No	No
Mervar & Hiebert	1989	2	Yes	No
Michalove	1989	2	No	Yes
Mills	1986	Preschool,K	No	No
Pierce	1984	2	No	No
Ribowsky	1986	K	Yes	No
Rowe	1987	Preschool	No	No
Shockley	1989	1	No	Yes
Short	1985	1	No	No
Stephens	1986	Special Education	No	Yes
Stephens & Harste	1985	1	No	Yes
Stice & Bertrand	1989	1,2	Yes	Yes
Teale & Martinez	1987	K	No	No
White, Vaughan, & Rorie	1986	1	No	Yes
Willert & Kamii	1985	K	No	No

[1]A study in which whole language was compared with traditional instruction.
[2]A study which included children considered to be at risk of school failure.

In addition to answering the specific questions raised by each researcher, the studies help readers understand how children learn in whole language classrooms. They report differences between learning in whole language and traditional classrooms, and document the role of the teacher in whole language classrooms.

Understanding Learning in Whole Language Classrooms

Myna Haussler (1982) and Mary Willert and Constance Kamii (1985) document the strategies children use as they learn to read and write. JoBeth Allen and Emily Carr (1989), Jean Anne Clyde (1987), Patricia Cousins (1988), Barbara Michalove (1989), Deborah Wells Rowe (1986), Betty Shockley (1989), and Kathy Gagne Short (1985) examine strategies within the social context and detail how the children learn from each other and from their teachers. JoBeth Allen (1988), Lee Dobson (1988), and Heidi Mills (1986) consider the relationship between reading and writing, and show how growth in one area supports growth in the other. June McConaghy (1986) is interested in how literature helps children "come to understand themselves and their world" and provides a close look at the learning of first-grade children from their teachers's perspective.

Working with teachers during a year in which they changed their instructional strategies, Virginia Pierce (1984) and Diane Stephens (1986) each examine student response and student growth relative to those changes. Kathy Short (1985) uses intertextuality as a metaphor for learning and examines how students and teachers learned from each other, as well as from past, present, and future texts.

Comparing Learning

The comparative studies consider how experiences in whole language classrooms compare with those in more traditional classrooms. Freppon used Burke's *Reading Interview* (1987) to ask first-grade children about reading and readers. Children in both whole language and traditional classrooms identified themselves as "good readers." However, those in traditional classrooms said they were good readers because they knew a lot of words; children in whole language classrooms said they were good readers because they read a lot of books. In addition, Freppon noted that, by year's end, more children in the whole language classroom developed an understanding of reading as a meaning-making process, reported using a greater variety of reading strategies, and were observed as doing so. More children from the whole language classroom also talked of using meaning to self-monitor their reading. Freppon concluded that children in the whole language classroom were more actively involved as readers.

Stice and Bertrand (in press) found that at-risk minority children in first and second grades performed "as well or better than their matches in traditional classrooms" on the Stanford Achievement Test, made more progress on the Clay's Concepts About Print (1979) test, retold longer, more complete versions of stories, "had greater awareness of alternative (reading) strategies, focused more on the meaning and communicative nature of language," and were more independent readers and writers. Stice and Bertrand also noted that "ninety-five percent of the whole language children report 'me' when asked, 'Who do you know who is a good reader?' Only five percent of the traditional children reported themselves."

Mervar and Hiebert (1989) reported that second-grade "low-achieving students in the literature-based classroom displayed literature selection strategies similar to those of their high-achieving peers and they read extensively." Hagerty, Hiebert and Owens (1989) noted that on the comprehension measure the fourth- and sixth-grade students in literature-based classrooms "outperformed those in skills-oriented classrooms" . . . and that students in the literature-based classrooms were better able to "verbalize the processes and strategies of reading and writing." In addition, from fall to spring, students' perceptions in the literature-based classroom moved from a skills– to a meaning–based view of reading and writing.

Understanding Teaching

Community is a consistent thread in the whole language classrooms included in this bibliography. The teachers surround the children with literacy experiences, help them understand the usefulness of literacy, invite them to participate in literacy experiences, and support their learning through demonstration, response, and strategic intervention. While many of the collaborative studies document this curricular process (Clyde, 1987; Cousins, 1988; Pierce, 1984; Stephens, 1986; Short, 1985), Carole Edelsky, Kelly Draper, and Karen Smith (1983) specifically examined curriculum making in one whole language teacher's classroom. To understand the decision-making process, they observed, interviewed, audiotaped, and videotaped the beginning of the year in Karen Smith's sixth-grade, inner-city classroom. As a result of data analysis, they identified goals that Smith had set for her classroom (including "to get students to see opportunities everywhere for learning" and "to get students to think and take pleasure in their intellects"); rules, roles, and cues that enabled her to reach those goals; and a set of values that guided her decision making. Many of Smith's goals, rules, roles, and cues are similar to those identified as characteristics of teachers in other whole language studies: She "modeled how to be," "structured the environment and curriculum to provide cues," conversed and collaborated, and colluded with students in order to reach her goals. However, most striking, perhaps, is one cue that appears to be common to all the whole language classroom research cited in this book. It also may be the most powerful and least labeled part of what Smith and other whole language teachers offer: Smith "behaved as if the desired were actual." Smith consistently "believed—and was observed behaving as if—the students were competent, sensible and well-intentioned." In describing the first day of school, for example, Edelsky, Draper, and Smith note:

> During the first three hours of school, children's timing seemed to be slightly "out of sync" as they looked around the room and to each other for guidance. Few answered questions; none ventured opinions. Nevertheless, during the first hour when Karen Smith (believing as if they could) gave them a copy of the same complicated time schedule she gave us, with the time blocks filled in for each day of the week, and told them to change the Tuesday 9:40-10:30 block from Directed Writing Activity to Writing Process, they rose to the occasion. Some of these poor readers glanced around quickly but then "got hold of themselves"; all made at least some kind of mark somewhere on their copy of the schedule. Three hours later they were having conversations with the teacher, cleaning up materials unasked, wondering aloud about scientific principles, and generally making themselves "at home" in the room.

Edelsky, Draper, and Smith concluded that "by the end of the first school day, these children (many of whom had failed two different grades already . . . several of whom had reputations as 'bad kids') looked like self-directed, conscientious 'good kids.'"

Directions for Future Research

These research studies illustrate how children in whole language classrooms access what Heap (1989) refers to as "rational literacy"; they know how to use reading and writing to learn, and they choose to do so. The studies also demonstrate how, in whole language classrooms, learning language in school parallels learning language outside of school. They provide evidence that teachers in whole language classrooms are informed, empowered practitioners.

There are, however, "holes" in the documentation and understanding of whole language classrooms and of the students and teachers who learn in them. Most of the studies cited here have been conducted in preschool, kindergarten, and first-grade environments. While there are a few studies of classrooms at other levels, we need more information about higher elementary, secondary, and special education whole language settings. Similarly, little research has been conducted on whole language classrooms at the college and university level. Much of the research has also been broad in scope (year-long qualitative studies, for example) and, within that, has focused on one or two particular aspects of the curriculum. There are many aspects that as yet are unexplored.

Annotated
Bibliography

Annotations of Case Study Research

Allen, J., Michalove, B., West, M., and Shockley, B. (1989). *Studying the Students We Worry About: A Collaborative Investigation of Literacy Learning.* Paper presented at the annual meeting of the National Reading Conference, Austin, TX.

Nine teachers from one elementary school (Fowler Elementary) took a summer course on whole language with JoBeth Allen. At the end of the course, they began to discuss the changes they intended to make the following year and ways to study the effectiveness of those changes. Based on their discussion, Allen issued an invitation to the faculty at Fowler Elementary. She would be offering an "inservice seminar on whole language, to be held at the school throughout the year." As a part of this seminar, participants would be observing and discussing children they were "worried about." Teachers interested in extending the observations into a research project could form a research team. Allen also indicated her interest in collaborating with teachers in their classrooms.

Seven teachers formed the Fowler Drive Research Team; three of them (Shockley, Michalove, and West) as collaborators with Allen. In their initial research meetings, the team identified children they were particularly worried about and selected three children to study from the classrooms of Shockley, Michalove, and West. Allen observed in each classroom one day per week. Another member of the research team, Sherie Gibney, videotaped each teacher at the beginning and middle of the year. She then viewed the tape with the teacher and interviewed the teacher about what had been taped.

In addition, teachers kept daily teaching journals in which they recorded observations about the three children. They also collected samples of children's writing and kept reading records for each child. The reading records included notes on the books children read and tapes of children's oral reading. Children were interviewed four times a year about "what they were learning as reader and writers, how they were learning, what they planned to learn next, and how they planned to learn." Additional data included pen pal letters that the children wrote to college

24

students, test scores, transcripts of interviews with parents and other teachers, and a research journal kept by Allen.

Data analysis involved weekly meetings, narrative synthesis documents written during the year, and case study reports written after the year had ended. To prepare the case study reports, members of the research team first read all the data for each child, making notes, and identifying possible issues, themes, and categories. Then they began a series of focused reading to fine-tune and cross-check these patterns.

Allen notes that engagement and community were themes that emerged across all nine case studies: "The children that 'worried' us at the beginning of the year were often those who were either not engaging with literacy events, or children who had non-productive roles within the literate community." She adds: "engagement came for all of the first and second grade students in our study, but at different points in the year, and through different routes . . . We are less certain about the three fifth grade students." Noting, however, the progress made by all children within the classroom community, Allen raises questions about the children's continuing literacy growth: "What will happen when this supportive classroom community breaks up? When children have learned to learn from a friend and that friend is no longer in the same room?"

The research team will continue to study the first- and second-grade children in order to address these kinds of questions.

Avery, C. (1985). Lori 'Figures It Out': A Young Writer Learns to Read. In J. Hansen, T. Newkirk, and D. Graves (Eds.), *Breaking Ground: Teachers Relate Reading and Writing in the Elementary School*. Portsmouth, NH: Heinemann.

This is a first-grade teacher's study of Lori, a child Avery describes as "average," "anxious," and "apprehensive" at the beginning of the year. Avery documents Lori's considerable reading and writing growth throughout the year with examples of her work and comments from interviews and journals. She also provides a description of her "learning process classroom," including such details as lesson planning, room organization, and assessment strategies. The study suggests that Lori and her peers benefited

25

from this integrated approach to learning: "In mid-December the class took the Level 2 test (of the Scott-Foresman Reading Program). A score of 45 was considered passing. The range in the class was 46 to 50 and nine students, including Lori, scored a perfect 50." Avery notes that, in her previous years of teaching, she had consistently administered the test later in the year and that scores frequently "dipped in the low 40's." On the California Achievement Test administered in May, the scores of the students ranged from the 76th to the 99th percentile. Avery notes that Lori not only scored at the 93rd percentile but also had become an "avid reader" who "had assumed responsibility for and control of her own learning process."

Barone, D., and Lovell, J. (1987). Bryan the Brave: A Second Grader's Growth as Reader and Writer. *Language Arts, 64,* 505–515.

This case study traces the writing and reading development of a second grade child. Bryan learned to see himself in literature and to write to a specific audience. The authors suggest that the opportunity to participate in a "richly interactive reading and writing environment," coupled with teacher belief and extensive peer response, contributed to the child's growth as a writer.

Boutwell, M. (1983). Reading and Writing: A Reciprocal Agreement. *Language Arts, 60,* 723–730.

Boutwell reflects on the reciprocal nature of the reading and writing process in her classroom, and reports on a case study of one of her students, a third grader. The article conveys a sense of the whole language classroom from the teacher's perspective, as well as the cognitive processes and learning strategies from the student's perspective.

Church, S., and Newman, J. (1985). Danny: A Case History of an Instructionally Induced Reading Problem. In J. Newman (Ed.), *Whole Language: Theory in Use.* Portsmouth, NH: Heinemann.

The case study discusses Danny, a ninth-grade boy from a middle-class family who was having reading difficulties. The

26

student's school history indicated that he had been in skill-oriented reading programs. In the beginning of the ninth grade, Danny participated in an instructional program that was based on a constructive model of reading. The program was designed to encourage the student to use semantic, syntactic, and grapho-phonemic cues. The researchers note that, at the end of the first year, Danny had become a much more strategic reader, was more willing to take risks as a reader, and was more interested in choosing to read. Danny also passed all his classes, and, in spite of the fact that he received no direct skill instruction, his scores on the Woodcock-Johnson test rose from 2.6 to 4.6

Crowley, P. (in process). *Readers' Views of the Reading Process, Their Own Reading and Reading Curriculum in a Whole Language School* (working title). Unpublished doctoral dissertation, University of Missouri, Columbia, MO.

This study investigates the views of students in a whole language school regarding the reading process, their own reading strategies, and the reading curriculum, including basal reader activities and literature discussion groups. Participants were identified by their teachers as readers of high, average, and low proficiency in grades 1–5. Using miscue analysis procedures and metacognitive reporting, participants' metacognitive awareness is examined in light of their reading strategies.

Five, C. (1985). Teresa: A Reciprocal Learning Experience for Teacher and Child. In J. Harste and D. Stephens (Eds.), *Toward Practical Theory*. Bloomington, Indiana University, Language Education Department.

Five, a fifth-grade teacher, examines the progress of one of her students, eleven-year-old Teresa. Teresa was labeled as learning disabled, and, based on data provided by test results and reports of other teachers, Five originally considered her "hopeless." At the beginning of the year, and consistent with previous years, Teresa was scheduled to leave the regular classroom for most of the day in order to work with an aide. She returned to Five's classroom only for art, music, and gym and to work on the worksheets assigned by the aide. This "worksheet" time corresponded

27

with writing, social studies, and science in Five's classroom. During the year, Teresa became a more active participant in these learning events. She began to find ways to stay in the room with the rest of the children. "By late Spring," Five reports, "Teresa became much more assertive and often refused to leave the class to work with her aide."

Five documents Teresa's metamorphosis from a shy, unrisking, unsuccessful child to one who was proud of her writing and eager to experiment and to explore. At year's end, Teresa, a successful learner, had developed confidence in her ideas and had "learned to express those ideas through art, discussion, simulation, manipulation, reading, and writing," Five hypothesizes:

> Teresa's aide did not allow her to take risks. There was no opportunity for experimenting and exploring. The curriculum for the learning disabled has very specific skill-oriented goals for students like Teresa. The emphasis was on what the student cannot do and what he or she does not know. It does not build on prior experience or abilities. It does not engage students in different strategies for learning. The curriculum for these special children lets them be learning disabled, and perhaps keeps them disabled. . . . A comprehension-centered, supportive environment seems to let Teresa be a successful learner—severely labeled perhaps, but not severely disabled. This type of environment builds on what she can do and respects her as an individual. It encourages ownership of ideas and responsibility for learning. From this sense of control comes independence.

Michalove, B. (1989). *Engagement and Community in a Second Grade Classroom.* Paper presented at the thirty-ninth annual meeting of the National Reading Conference, Austin, TX.

As part of a university-public school collaborative research project (*see* Allen, et al., 1989, on page 24), Michalove studied three black children from low-income families, all second graders who had already repeated a year of school. Two of the children had behavior problems: Reggie was highly social, had trouble staying still, and had become a disruptive force in the classroom; Ricky was aggressive and asocial; Lee was identified as mentally handicapped and spent two hours a day in the resource room.

Michalove documents the progress that the three children made as readers and writers. She notes that Reggie learned to read and that it was two of his classmates who taught him to do so. Initially reluctant to write, by year's end he was "so engaged with his writing it was hard to get him to shift gears when we had to move him to another subject." Ricky, who came into second grade as a reader, initially lacked confidence but became a confident reader over the course of the year. As a writer, he began by sitting alone, copying from other books. Over the course of the year, he started to collaborate with other children. His confidence grew, and he began to write "about some parts of his life outside of school. He also wrote summaries, new versions and personal opinions about the books he was reading." Lee, who at the beginning of the year "hadn't yet developed the concept that a group of letters stands for a word," asked at the end of the year "if he could read one of his well-learned books to his first grade teacher's class . . ." and wrote a note to the teacher, Ms. Williams, asking permission to do so.

Michalove concludes:

> By allowing the children to use their individual strengths, they "learned how to learn" using all the resources available. Hopefully, their involvement in this community will contribute to reducing risks for their continued success. It did not provide an instant cure. Lee still reads below grade level, but the progress he made raises the question of his label of retardation. Ricky describes himself as shy; that he will describe himself at all is a big step for him. Although Reggie continues to struggle with reading, his image of himself as a reader is drastically different. Let me share with you a section of a piece of writing his older brother wrote this fall: "My brother named Reggie want to go to the place called the White House to see President Bush in Washington, D.C. because he want to read to him."

Shockley, B. (1989). *Sing a Song of Joseph*. Paper presented at the thirty-ninth annual meeting of the National Reading Conference, Austin, TX.

Shockley was a member of a university-public school research team (*see* Allen, et al., 1989, on page 24) that conducted case studies on children they "worried" about. In this paper, she reports on Joseph, a first grader who already had spent an extra year in a special needs kindergarten. Labeled both mildly mentally handicapped and behaviorally disordered, Joseph had been placed in Shockley's classroom after having been removed from another first-grade classroom because of "aggressive and disruptive" behavior.

In the context of Joseph's frequent problems with inappropriate behavior, Shockley details his growth as a reader and writer over the course of the year. She notes, for example, that at the beginning of the year "he could only write his name. . . . He participated in writing workshop by writing letters, drawing pictures and telling his picture story." By February 7th, he had progressed to writing a "patterned dialogue" story, using words he was sure he knew how to spell correctly. He made similar progress in reading, moving through both preprimers to the point that on the last day of class he read a page in the last story of the second preprimer to the class.

Shockley notes that, by year's end, Joseph no longer had "to solely rely on his tough guy image to gain respect but (could) legitimately participate in academic endeavors." She cautions, however, that "as he learns, he reduces his risks but does not erase them." Joseph continues to live in "complex worlds of choices, models and expectations which are often in conflict with one another."

Shockley details some of those experiences: a brother who put glue on the eyes and mouth of a hamster and then watched it walk around until it died, police coming to the house to arrest another brother, four cousins who died because of a faulty space heater, stepbrothers who moved in with Joseph because their father had abused them.

Making connections with a day when Joseph pulled his own tooth in the bathroom (and found out from Shockley about the tooth fairy), Shockley concludes:

> Even though he made impressive literacy leaps, it is not clear that such skills will be enough support for life outside of Fowler Drive School, or even outside my classroom. . . . How could this be enough when he was consistently confused by input from brothers and cousins—people he really

cared about and admired? . . . When he was angry one afternoon, he threatened, "I'll scratch a teacher just like my brother do if she make me mad. . . ."

But perhaps most telling of all are the times when his innocence about "usual" childhood experiences became apparent. For instance, during our trip to the university (which Joseph referred to as a "white people's place"), one of the students put a coin in the fountain and made a wish. A few days later in class Joseph asked, "Those wishes come true at that place?" He held up a quarter for me.

The school system is granting Joseph some of his wishes. However, as citizens and educators, maybe we need to get the tooth fairy to come before we expect miracles from ourselves and our children in these complex times and worlds.

Stephens, D., and Harste, J. (1985). Accessing the Potential of the Learner: Towards an Understanding of the Complexities of Context. *Peabody Journal of Education, 62,* 86–99.

This article examines the literacy behaviors of a first-grade child across the contexts of home, school, and clinic. The assessment of the child's learning difficulties is detailed, and the value of a supportive, learning-centered environment is explored. The authors suggest that such an environment contributed significantly to the child's eventual progress as a reader and a writer.

Annotations of Classroom Studies

Allen, J. (1988). *Literacy Development in Whole Language Kindergartens* (Technical Report No. 436). Urbana-Champaign, IL: University of Illinois, Center for the Study of Reading.

As part of the Whole Language Literacy Program in their school district, seven teachers spent a year studying the literacy development of the children in their whole language kindergartens. Allen notes that "no children were excluded from the study. There were children with identified or suspected learning problems, language delays of up to two and a half years, children who were repeating

kindergarten and those with probable emotional strains. . . ."
During the year, the teachers kept observational records, collected
writing samples, completed questionnaires and a Types-of-
Writing-Produced form quarterly, and assessed each child's reading in September and then again in May. They met each week with
a university collaborator, first to design the study and then to
share observations and to identify patterns in the data.

Findings suggest that 95 percent of the children made progress as writers. The children became more conventional in their
writing and also expanded the types of writing they did. Allen
reports that this writing development was "not a stair-stepped
sequence. . . . Rather, children became more flexible in their
use of an increasing number of literacy strategies."

Allen also reports that "children improved their ability to
make connections between sounds and letters in words they
were reading as they learned to represent words on paper." Cor-
relational data from this study suggest that "entry level did not
determine exit level; most children made progress regardless of
where they started in either reading or writing."

Allen, J., and Carr, E. (1989). Collaborative Learning Among
    Kindergarten Writers: Jamie Learns How to Read at School.
    In J. Allen and J. Mason (Eds.), *Risk Makers, Risk Takers, Risk
    Breakers: Reducing the Risks for Young Literacy Learners.*
    Portsmouth, NH: Heinemann.

In this collaborative study, Allen and Carr analyze transcripts
from writing sessions, written products, and interview protocols
in order to understand how twenty-one kindergarten children
(twelve black and nine white) taught and learned from each
other. Focusing their analysis on one hundred and six instructional episodes, the researchers conclude that "children became
better teachers, as well as better learners, over time. . . . [T]hey
became better teachers in part by emulating the adult models,
and in part by the way their peers responded to and thus shaped
their teaching moves." Reporting on interviews with the children, Allen and Carr note that "almost all of them identified
other children when asked who was helping them learn to read
and write. They also recognized that they helped other children
in the class. . . ." The researchers note that literacy learning in

the classroom was a social activity and that, through interactions, children were learning not only specific literacy skills but also how to "do school."

Within the broader study, the researchers use a case study to focus on one child's experience over the course of the year and document his growth as reader, writer, and learner.

Brabson, C. (in process). *The Kinds of Anomalies Encountered While Participating in Literacy Events and the Environmental Conditions That Support Anomalies.* Unpublished doctoral dissertation, Indiana University, Bloomington, IN.

Brabson was interested in understanding the role of anomalies in the literacy learning of special education students. She defined an anomaly as an event recognized by individuals as somehow violating the prediction that was part of their ongoing experience. Anomalies emerge when an individual knows what to predict and recognizes that something has gone wrong. Three questions guided her data collection: (1) What kinds of anomalies do special education students encounter when participating in literacy events? (2) What strategies do they use in attempting to create meaning in these anomalous situations? (3) What are the conditions and characteristics of the environment that support the emergence of anomalous situations?

Preliminary findings suggest that continuity of experience plays an important role in the educational process. If special education students encounter anomalous events that form a dysfunction between home and school experiences, school experiences are often miseducative.

Clyde, J. A. (1987). *A Collaborative Venture: Exploring the Sociopsycholinguistic Nature of Literacy.* Unpublished doctoral dissertation, Indiana University, Bloomington, IN.

Clyde spent one spring semester helping the staff at the Campus Children's Center incorporate research on how children learn to read and write into their program. The following year she and the teachers began to examine how the curriculum supported the preschool children as learners. Her study first details the collaborative curriculum-building process, documenting the events through which she and the teachers developed a theoretical frame to guide decision making. Working together, the teachers (including Clyde) decided that "each literacy experience would ideally (1) be inherently social . . . , (2) offer opportunities for all language users . . . to provide demonstrations for one another . . . , (3) feature choice . . . , (4) offer participants an opportunity to shift psychological stance . . . , (5) allow the four systems of language to transact naturally . . . and, (6) have the potential to generate invitations to literacy that might extend beyond the classroom into the children's out-of-school lives." They also made the decision to be participants with the children—"to read, write, sing, dance, finger paint, build with blocks, count, clean, and anything else that the children did— right alongside them."

As a part of their research efforts, Clyde and the teachers identified key language settings (mailboxes, a message board, and the children's newspaper), detailed data collection techniques, and, as means of self-correction, committed themselves to keeping personal diaries, to team debriefing, to providing each other with feedback on a daily basis, and to using the children as "research and curricular informants."

Using language events to illustrate their findings, Clyde's text offers insight into the learning that occurred for children, for teachers, and for the curriculum and community that evolved. Clyde emphasizes that the children in the study came to "believe that reading and writing constitute a form of social action, are intentional and involve the making and sharing of meaning. . . . These children [saw] literacy as functional, a vehicle through which they [could] explore and expand their world, a tool of getting things done." She notes that the "three- and four-year-olds engage[d] in literacy activity as easily and naturally as they [did] any other sort of learning."

The language events, coupled with case studies of four learners, illustrate the children's use of print to negotiate their world. Clyde documents the literacy explorations of children, showing their growth as language users, highlighting the functional uses children made of print and of children's awareness both of what they knew and of what they wanted to learn next about language. The study details the process of teaching through demonstration and closely examines how children learn about written language from their teachers and each other.

Cousins, P. (1988). *The Social Construction of Learning Problems: Language Use in a Special Education Classroom.* Unpublished doctoral dissertation, Indiana University, Bloomington, IN.

Alane Lancaster is a teacher in a resource room for students identified as learning disabled or mildly mentally handicapped. At the time of the study, her district had developed, and was about to implement, a language arts program that "focused on having students read and write for real purposes." Patricia Cousins was a doctoral student interested in the relationship between learning, reflection, language, and curriculum in classrooms for special learners. They collaborated for an academic year, working to implement the new curriculum and to understand the role of language in learning. This study discusses their collaboration, details both their curriculum and their research, and then focuses on students' use of language.

Cousins uses choice, interest, reflection, and participation to characterize classroom events and concludes that language use was strongly affected by the characteristics of particular events. When events "involved choice, built upon student interest, included opportunities for reflection and evaluation and involved the teacher as participant," Cousins found that the students "used language to expand their present ideas . . . to explore what they currently knew . . . used a more diverse group of strategies . . . [and] tried out a diversity of roles, from teacher to learner." Cousins argues that "in the more traditionally structured events the students looked like and sounded like our stereotypes of special education students—they were 'off task' and their language was typically simplistic and minimal, while in other events, they looked like and sounded like proficient language users."

Her analysis suggests that traditional structures do not provide opportunities for students to use language to learn and that, within those traditional structures, students often use language for other purposes, such as playing out the role of student or using language to bypass reading and writing. Cousins concludes that teachers and students have developed ways of interacting that work against using language to learn and suggests that altering the classroom context (in the direction of choice, interest, participation, and collaborative structures) provides opportunities for students to develop and use productive literacy behaviors.

Dahl, K., and Freppon, P. (in process). *An Investigation of the Ways Low-SES Children in Whole Language Classrooms Make Sense of Instruction in Reading and Writing in the Early Grades.*

Dahl and Purcell-Gates (1989) conducted a two-year study to understand how thirty-six children in three traditional, skills-based classrooms, kindergarten through grade 1, made sense of reading and writing instruction. Analysis of the data from the kindergarten year (Dahl, 1988) suggests that during teacher-directed activities, learners across three sites "spent the bulk of their time following the teacher's directions. They copied letters, marked answers and replied to the teachers' questions." However, during self-sponsored activities, "learners experimented with written language. . . . Instead of answering questions, the learners asked questions. They explored the stuff of literacy— wrote names, handled books and talked about their problems with written language."

When children's hypotheses were contrasted across sites, it "became evident (that) learner actions reflected the curriculum they were experiencing. . . . If the curriculum led them to think of letters, they learned about letters—if it provided experience in various ways to attempt reading, that was what they learned."

Dahl and Purcell-Gates also examined hypotheses relative to the child's achievement level at the beginning of kindergarten. Results of that analysis suggest that "the high group seemed to move from interest in the functionality of written language to recognition of letters and the alphabetic principle and finally to various reading attempts. . . . In contrast, the low group remained concerned with letters and while they indicated some grasp of the alphabetic principle, they seemed to be interested in copying words rather than reading them."

The results of their first study revealed that, while "low-SES learners entered formal schooling with extremely limited knowledge of written language," the traditional curriculum incorrectly assumed that inner-city children understood the functionality of written language and thus dealt primarily with the "inner workings" of print (sound and symbol relationships, and so forth), resulting in a mismatch between learner knowledge and the curriculum marked. . . . Children became instructionally dependent."

Their current research builds on these earlier studies in an attempt to understand how low-SES children make sense of instruction in whole language classrooms and how these hypotheses compare with the hypotheses in the skills-based classrooms studied by Dahl and Purcell-Gates (1989).

DeFord, D. (1981). Literacy: Reading, Writing and Other Essentials. *Language Arts, 6,* 652–658.

Three first-grade classrooms, labeled as skills, phonics, and whole language, were observed for seven months in order to understand the effect of instruction on reading and writing strategies. DeFord's findings suggest that children's texts reflected instruction: In the skills classroom, they wrote sentences that contained words they had encountered (*Bill can run*); in the phonics classrooms, their sentences focused on the sounds they had learned (*ihddcat*—"I had a cat"); in the whole language classrooms, they wrote stories they wanted to tell (*Iran is fighting U.S.*).

DeLawter, J. (1975). The Relationship of Beginning Reading Instruction and Miscue Patterns. In W. Page (Ed.), *Help for the Reading Teacher: New Directions in Research.* Urbana, IL: National Council of Teachers of English.

The purpose of this study was to determine if there were differences in miscue patterns between children who received beginning reading instruction that emphasized decoding and one that emphasized meaning. The results of the study suggest that children taught by a meaning-oriented approach tend to make miscues that are semantically acceptable, while those taught with an emphasis on decoding produce nonword miscues.

37

Dobson, L. (1988). *Connections in Learning to Write and Read: A Study of Children's Development Through Kindergarten and Grade One* (Technical Report No. 418). Urbana-Champaign, IL: University of Illinois, Center for the Study of Reading.

This study traced the reading and writing development of eighteen children (many of whom were learning English as a second language) from kindergarten through first grade in an inner-city "integrated instructional program." Dobson analyzed the children's reading and writing in order to "identify common strategies and to compare their use across the tasks." The study documents "levels of understanding . . . of print awareness," which represent "a progression toward the conventional." Dobson notes that this progression was "continuous rather than stagelike" and that, while "the effect was cumulative . . . there were also shifts of priority and focus." Dobson notes further that, as the children developed as readers and writers, writing and reading "supported each other" and that there was a "transfer of strategies occurring in both directions."

(See also Dobson, L. (1983). *The Progress of Early Writers as They Discover Written Language for Themselves.* Vancouver, B.C.: Educational Research Institute of British Columbia, Report No. 83:11 (ERIC Document Reproduction Service No. ED 235, 505) and Dobson, L. (1985). Learn to Read by Writing: A Practical Program for Reluctant Readers. *Teaching Exceptional Children, 18,* 30–36.)

Edelsky, C., Draper, K., and Smith, K. (1983). Hookin 'em in at the Start of School in a Whole Language Classroom. *Anthropology and Education Quarterly, 14,* 257–281.

Edelsky, Draper, and Smith point out that most studies of effective teaching are based on a skills model of teaching. Likewise, studies of the beginnings of the school year often seek to delineate what distinguishes effective from ineffective teachers, using a skills model of teaching. They suggest, however, that a skills model is typical, not inherent. To explore effective teaching from a whole language perspective, they investigated the opening weeks of school in an inner-city, sixth-grade classroom. They initially hypothesized that, over a period of several weeks, the students would make gradual changes in response to the whole language approach taken by their teacher. However, they discovered that the adaptation process occurred very rapidly and that, indeed, the students seemed very different, even at the end of the first day.

In order to determine how this had occurred, the researchers looked for patterns in the data and identified goals, values, rules, roles, and cues as salient characteristics. They noted that the teacher had a clear sense of what she wanted to accomplish:

1. To get students to see opportunities everywhere for learning.
2. To get students to think and take pleasure in using their intellects.
3. To help students learn to get along with and appreciate others.
4. To manage the day-to-day environment smoothly.
5. To get students to relate to and identify with the teacher.
6. To get them to be self-reliant and sure of themselves, and to trust their own judgment.

The researchers also noted that the decisions made by the teacher, Karen Smith, were guided by these goals and by a set of values. The researchers labeled these values as follows: Respect, People are Good, Interdependence, Independence, Activity and Work, and Originality. Edelsky, Draper, and Smith identified the implicit rules of the classroom ("Do exactly as I say," "Use your head," "Do what's effective," and "No cop-outs") and the roles that Smith played: Lesson Leader, Information Dispenser, Scout Leader, Consultant/Coach, Neutral Recorder, and Preacher. Smith utilized a variety of cues to communicate to the students her goals and values. "The cuing devices were: Using the work of others as examples, giving directions . . . , telling what not to do . . . , ignoring inappropriate behavior, reminding or checking up, behaving as if the desired were actual, modeling how to be, and structuring the environment and curriculum to provide the cues."

The description of how this teacher used roles, rules, and cues to reach her goals and establish her values contrasts sharply with the research on effective teaching in a skills classroom. Edelsky, Draper, and Smith suggest that the difference occurs because most of the research on effective teaching (1) assumes a skills model and so fails to consider that to which the students are adapting, and (2) evaluates effective teaching in terms of improvement on standardized test scores.

Freppon, P. (1988). *An Investigation of Children's Concepts of the Purpose and Nature of Reading in Different Instructional Settings.* Unpublished doctoral dissertation, University of Cincinnati, Cincinnati, OH.

Freppon identified four first-grade classrooms as two "literature based" and two "skills based." Controlling for socioeconomic status, gender, reading ability, and reading instruction, Freppon randomly selected twenty-four average readers and used "structured interviews . . . altered passages . . . and in-process oral reading behaviors" to access the students' beliefs and understandings about reading. The results of her study suggest that there were significant differences between the two groups and that those differences correlated with instruction. For example, when presented with semantically, syntactically, and lexically altered passages (e.g., "Wash and the boy are washing to he car rain"), "ninety-seven percent of the literature-based groups rejected the passages by identifying them as lacking language-like characteristics or as not being meaningful. Only forty-two percent of the skills-based group rejected the . . . altered passages."

Freppon also notes that "analysis of the presentations of altered passages yielded information on an affective response from the two groups of students. . . . Analysis . . . showed that eight of the twelve literature-based students laughed (often repeatedly) or exhibited other expressions of humor. . . . Two skill-based students exhibited signs of humor." She reports one literature-based student's comments: "Well! It's easy to read but this doesn't make *any* sense . . . (smiling playfully) Did *you* just type this up?"

Results from interview data also suggest differences between the two groups: "Ninety-two percent in the literature-based group said that understanding the story or both understanding and getting the words right is more important in reading . . . in the skills-based group, only fifty percent talked about both . . . as important in reading."

Freppon notes that the two groups of children also varied in the variety of strategies they used as readers, in their self-monitoring, in their understanding of a "good reader," and in their view of themselves as readers. For example, children in the literature-based group reported using more strategies and were observed to do so, and more often discussed using meaning to self-monitor. While children in both groups said that they were good readers, those in the literature-based groups said that they were good readers because they read a lot of books, whereas children in the skills group said they were good readers because they knew a lot of words.

Analysis of Running Records (Clay, 1972), used to identify patterns in oral reading, suggests that both groups of children had similar accuracy rates and had nearly equal rereading behaviors. The number of times they asked for help was also similar. Freppon reports, however, that there were also differences. The skills group "attempted to sound out words more than twice as often as did the literature group," and, when attempting to sound out, the literature group did so more successfully than did the skills group (success rates of 53 percent and 32 percent, respectively). There were also differences in the use of cue systems. Thirty-four percent of the time the students in the literature group used a "balanced cuing system, which meant they used meaning, structure and visual cues in making the substitutions. The skills group used a well-integrated or balanced cuing system 8 percent of the time."

Freppon argues that the results of this study suggest that the "literature-based group were more actively involved as readers in the process of constructing meaning in the reading process . . . [they] appeared to have understood the relationship between the parts of reading [the words and word decoding] and the purpose of the whole [to communicate meaningfully]. Simply put, these children seemed to have grasped the notion that reading is a language process." She adds: "They seemed to have acquired some of their understandings about the importance of words and sounding out words without traditional, sequenced instruction in vocabulary building and phonics."

In contrast, Freppon notes that, in the skills-based group, "the nature of the relationship of word-level aspects within the global, communicative purpose of reading did not seem well understood."

41

In her discussion, Freppon comments that "the students in the study were found to differ in significant ways which were not revealed through traditional reading assessment." She concludes that, while "both development and instruction play a part in shaping children's reading schemata . . . instruction appeared to be instrumental in shaping the reading schemata of young children."

Gunderson, L., and Shapiro, J. (1987). Some Findings on Whole Language Instruction. *Reading Canada Lecture, 5,* 22–26.

This study describes the educational activities of two first-grade classrooms in order to compare the differences between the whole language and basal instruction. The results suggest that children in the whole language program learned as much about phonics and vocabulary through reading and writing as did the other group through basal-based instruction.

Gunderson, L., and Shapiro, J. (1988). Whole Language Instruction: Writing in First Grade. *Reading Teacher, 41,* 430–439.

This article examines two first-grade whole language classrooms and discusses how various groups (e.g., writers and nonwriters) were guided into the learning process. The authors outline the curriculum that was in place and discuss the children's growth as readers and writers during the year.

Hagerty, P., Hiebert, E., and Owens, M. (1989). Students' Comprehension, Writing and Perceptions in Two Approaches to Literacy Instruction. In S. McCormick and J. Zutell (Eds.), *1989 National Reading Conference Yearbook.*

Hagerty, Hiebert, and Owens cite NAEP (National Assessment of Educational Progress) findings in noting that American school children "do poorly when tasks require application or problem-solving" and suggest that classrooms that emphasize "reading and writing as constructive processes" have the potential to improve children's problem-solving abilities. To understand the influence of such instruction, they identified classrooms at the second-, fourth-, and sixth-grade levels that promoted

42

"constructive, strategic processing." Hagerty, Hiebert, and Owens labeled these classrooms as whole language or literature based and compared them to traditional classrooms. Arguing for a broader view of literacy than that accessed through standardized test scores, the researchers analyzed reading comprehension and writing assessment test data, used a modification of Burke's *Reading Interview* (1987) to ask students how they thought about reading and writing, and observed in the classrooms.

The results of their study suggest that, on the comprehension test, "students in the literature-based classrooms outperformed those in skills-oriented classrooms." On the writing assessment task, there were no statistically significant differences between classes, although students in the fourth- and sixth-grade whole language classrooms scored approximately one standard deviation higher than the students in the traditional classrooms. Hagerty, Hiebert, and Owens note, however, that the writing assessment emphasized structure rather than fluency and measured ability to write on predetermined rather than self-selected topics. They suggest that measures which were more consistent with authentic uses of literacy might have resulted in differences that were consistently and statistically significant. Results from *Reading Interview* "favored the literature-based students." Over the course of the year, their perceptions about the role of literacy "shifted to emphasize the meaningful nature of reading and writing." Noting that these results "suggest that children's views mirror the view of instruction," Hagerty, Hiebert, and Owens suggest that "the relationship of these perceptions to students' futures as readers and writers is an important one for future research to consider."

Hanssen, E. (in process). *The Social Creation of Meaning: Learning as a Dialogic Process* (working title). Unpublished doctoral dissertation, Indiana University, Bloomington, IN.

Hanssen spent a year co-teaching with Carol Porter in three junior high language arts classes. Together they developed a curriculum in which students read, wrote, and talked about their reading and writing. The focus of the study was on these dialogues and on the type of meaning students made from and through their discussions.

Haussler, M. (1982). *Transitions into Literacy: A Psycholinguistic Analysis of Beginning Reading in Kindergarten and First Grade Children.* Unpublished doctoral dissertation: University of Arizona, Tucson, AZ.

A year-long study of eight children in Robert Wortman's whole-day kindergarten and first grade whole language classroom focused on the relationship of environment print awareness, book-handling knowledge, and metalinguistic awareness to beginning reading. Children were selected for the study if they had a beginning knowledge of print but were not considered readers by their parents or teachers. Four of these children were identified as having a high degree of environmental print awareness and four were identified as having a low degree of print awareness.

Data were collected throughout the year and consisted of a signs-of-the-environment and book-handling task, reading interviews, audiotaped reading sessions, teacher interviews, parent surveys, and monthly classroom observations.

The study details the literacy development of each of the eight children and notes that, by May, all children "were learning to deal with connected discourse and used a variety of integrated and non-integrated beginning reading strategies and transitional responses."

In reporting her results, Haussler offers these hypotheses:

1. All of the children were aware of print in context. This awareness increased from September to May. Some children used environmental print to begin reading, other children chose "other avenues . . . as transitions into the reading of connected discourse."

2. The children from "middle class families were able to respond more appropriately as print became more decontextualized than were subjects from working class families."

3. "Specific knowledge about books and book handling compared closely with the ability to effectively integrate reading strategies. . . . The subjects who became the best readers during the study demonstrated greater knowledge of: use of book, reading of print, and teacher register. Students who continued using transitional reading strategies throughout

demonstrated much less knowledge of reading print in connected text and teaching register."

4. "Subjects' knowledge of the teaching register as is measured by some aspects of the book-handling task relates more closely to their success in reading than does metalinguistic awareness. In other words, being able to use school register or school language in appropriate situations appears to be more related to beginning school reading than showing overt evidence of analyzing one's own language processing."

5. "Children use a variety of reading cues and strategies which are not specifically taught to them. Among these are the strategies of prediction, confirmation and correction."

6. "When five- and six-year-olds who have had experience with connected discourse attempt to read a new text, they use a number of transitional reading responses to gain meaning. These include semantic use of picture, knowledge of the structure of language (English), 'sense of story,' metalinguistic awareness or metacognition and integration of some print cues. . . . When these same transitional readers attempt to read text with which they are familiar, they also employ the transitional response of holistic remembering. Holistic remembering is an integration of semantic use of pictures, children's own knowledge of language in books, and their experience with a given text. Holistic remembering is called reading-like behavior by Doake (1985) and Holdaway (1979)."

7. "Children begin to read text effectively when they integrate the three language cuing systems (semantic, syntactic and graphophonic) and knowledge of reading books, such as using picture cues, sense of story and left to right directionality."

Summarizing across the year-long study, Haussler concludes:

Although children can learn to read without instruction, they cannot learn to read solely on their own. They learn about written language in a manner similar to which they learn to listen and speak. They learn through interaction and experience with others in their homes and communities, as is demonstrated in this study. Children who have a variety of print experiences are the most environmentally print aware. Most children with early book experiences have the most book-handling knowledge and are also the best readers. . . . Providing interactive experiences for children to read and supplying contextual supports as well as emotional support are essential for transitions into literacy.

McConaghy, J. (1986). *Literature, Literacy and Young Children.* Unpublished master's thesis, University of Alberta, Edmonton, Canada.

McConaghy conducted a two-year observational study in her first-grade literature-based classroom in order to understand how the children engaged with, and responded to, literature. She particularly wanted to know how young children "come to understand themselves and their world through reading and writing literature." Children's writing samples and their oral and written responses to literature were analyzed to identify patterns. The students spent a considerable amount of time choosing to read and write, and McConaghy's results suggest that they learned about reading and writing as part of that engagement. McConaghy's results further suggest that:

1. "Young children . . . link their lives to a story in such a way that reading literature [becomes] a meaning making experience."

2. "Children often ask to hear the same story read over and over and during the rereadings, children make comments on different parts of the story."

3. Learning occurs even when the teacher is not instructing.

4. Retellings provide the children with a different way of "knowing, understanding and savoring" stories.

5. Children frequently designed their own follow-up activities.

6. Talking about the story first often helped the child "go beyond the story itself and think about his own experience."

7. Children had "a very strong desire to talk about the books and stories they were reading."

8. Not all children experienced reading and writing literature in the same way. (These experiences can be categorized as literal, role playing, and transcending the text.)

9. Much of the children's writing "strongly reflected the influence of literature."

10. While they were writing, children learned different things about writing at different times.

McConaghy also noted that the children's experiences with literature provided them the opportunity to explore things in their world, "to engage in problem solving . . . to build meaning and to begin to understand some of the complexities of human nature."

Mervar, K. and Hiebert, E. (1989). Literature Selection Strategies and Amount of Reading in Two Literacy Approaches. In S. McCormick and J. Zutell (Eds.), *1989 National Reading Conference Yearbook.*

Mervar and Hiebert cite Kirsch and Jungeblut (1986) in noting that there is reason to question whether "many individuals have the necessary literacy skills to be full participants in workplaces and communities where the ability to interpret, synthesize and evaluate large quantities of information is a necessity." They argue that teaching for the standardized test may have acerbated the problem and that "the criteria for evaluating effective school literacy programs need to include characteristics of proficient readers that are not now part of typical assessments." To this end, they examined "the success of two literacy approaches in developing two . . . attributes of proficient readers: extensive participation in reading and literature selection strategies."

Twenty second-grade children—ten from a literature-based reading and ten from a skills-oriented classroom—participated in this study. Mervar and Hiebert observed the children in class and in the library, interviewed them about their behaviors, analyzed their reading logs, and asked them to rank-order a set of books, starting with the "best" one.

The results of their study suggest that, in school, students in the literature-based program read more than the students in the traditional program. High-achieving students in the literature-based program read more than three times the number of words (22,731 versus 6,805) than did their counterparts in the traditional classrooms. Low-achieving students in the literature-based program also read more than their peers in the traditional classroom: 8,384 versus 4,643 words. There were no significant differences in the number of books the two groups read or in two ability levels of students reported reading at home. Nor were there any "patterns for the rankings of either group" on the book-ranking task.

Differences were noted in book selection. Students in the literature-based classrooms reported more strategies for choosing texts and were also observed to use more strategies. As Mervar and Hiebert note, "The pattern of book selection for students in the skills-oriented classroom was to go to one part of the library which contained familiar books and immediately pull a book from the shelf. These books became their selection for the week. With no exceptions, all children in the literature-based classroom sampled text from one of more books before making their selections, either by reading parts of books to themselves or to another child. They also employed strategies like using the card catalog to find books on a desired topic or author."

Mills, H. (1986). *Writing Evaluation: A Transactional Process.* Unpublished doctoral dissertation, Indiana University, Bloomington, IN.

Mills worked for two years as a teacher-researcher in a preschool and kindergarten program that was affiliated with the public school system. Her study begins with a discussion of the theoretical foundation on which the curriculum was built and moves to a description of the curriculum used, of a typical day, and of the decision-making process of the teachers. Within this context, Mills then explores the children's growth as readers and writers. She analyzes the literacy growth of three children and, as she does so, develops categories for writing evaluation.

Summarizing across all three case studies, Mills concludes that:

1. Writing development is a transactive process that involves the refinement of many skills and strategies simultaneously.

48

2. Although all three children evidenced tremendous growth, their paths were diverse.
3. Flexible use of strategies led to empowerment.
4. The potential of a quality literacy activity was realized over time.

Mills then develops a framework for writing evaluation that is consistent with a process approach at the preschool and kindergarten level. She begins by listing salient characteristics of the literacy development of the children in her study and by providing examples of each. She suggests that teachers "record observations in process and collect corresponding artifacts" and then use the categories she has developed to reflect upon the significance of those records. Mills argues that it is critical for teachers to document their reflections and use the insights gained to inform instruction. She advocates an evaluation cycle through which teachers collect data, reflect, record, evaluate, and then make "new plans and invitations" for literacy experiences.

Pierce, V. (1984). *Bridging the Gap Between Language Research/ Theory and Practice: A Case Study.* Unpublished doctoral dissertation, Texas Woman's University, Denton, TX.

Pierce conducted a year-long classroom-based study in order to understand the effect of teacher-researcher collaboration on teacher and classroom change. Pierce spent the initial three months as observer, seeking to understand the practices and decision making of two second-grade teachers. In the second phase, from January to April, she became both facilitator and disseminator, planning, conducting, and carrying out collaborative planning sessions that focused on natural language learning. During the third phase, in May, she resumed the primary role of observer. Using field notes, interviews, materials gathered on site, and Deford's Theoretical Orientation to Reading Profile, Pierce examined both teacher and student changes.

Her study suggests that, during the collaborative phase of the study, the teachers assumed more control of the curriculum and began to see themselves as capable decision makers. They made substantial changes in their curriculum, altered their teaching style, began to evidence an appreciation of the

49

children's developing reading and writing skills and strategies, and revised their perspective on literacy and teaching. As the teachers made these changes, the students became more interested in, and involved with, reading and writing tasks. They became so enthusiastic that, as one of the teachers suggested when the students were working on reading and writing, "it's like they are having art." The students also assumed greater responsibility for working independently and often chose literacy activities as things they wanted to do, not only during the school day, but also after school and during the summer.

Examples of student work are used to demonstrate student growth as readers and writers; both classes also showed a two-year gain on standardized achievement test scores. In addition, Pierce compared scores on end-of-year standardized tests and found that the students in these two classrooms scored above the school and district mean, as well as above the mean of the students from a school with a similar population.

Ribowsky, H. (1986). *The Comparative Effects of a Code Emphasis Approach and a Whole Language Approach upon Emergent Literacy of Kindergarten Children.* Unpublished doctoral dissertation, New York University, NY.

This year-long study compared the effects of a code emphasis approach and a whole language approach on the emergent literacy of fifty-three kindergarten girls. According to the author, this is the first quantitative study of the whole language approach (*see* End Note on page 57). The subjects of the study were from two kindergarten classes from a parochial school in the Northeast.

The experimental class received instruction in Holdaway's Shared Book Experience Program (1979): (1) welcoming activity: reading aloud of poem, chant, or song; use of enlarged material; (2) favorite stories: rereading of stories, usually by request; unison participation; discussion of syntax; (3) language activity: exploration of language through games, riddles, puzzles; (4) new story: introduction of new story for the day; words pointed to as they are read aloud; language experiences shared; (5) independent reading: self-selection of books to read; engagement in literary activities of choice; (6) expression: art and writing activities; group drama.

The comparison class was instructed with a code emphasis approach using Lippincott's Beginning to Read, Write, and Listen Program.

Emergent literacy was the major dependent variable in the study. The emergent literacy factors analyzed were linguistic, orthographic, and graphophonemic literacy. "ANCOVA results revealed a significant main effect for treatment favoring the whole language group on all dependent measures." The results corroborated Holdaway's (1979) ethnographic research findings.

Ribowsky concluded that "a whole language approach was more effective than a code emphasis in fostering emergent literacy." She noted that shared book experiences strongly contributed to emergent literacy and that "literacy development occurred along developmental pathways unique to each child."

Rowe, D. W. (1987). Literacy Learning as an Intertextual Process. In J. E. Readence and R. S. Baldwin (Eds.), *Research in Literacy: Merging Perspectives. Thirty-sixth Yearbook of the National Reading Conference.* Rochester, NY: National Reading Conference.

The purpose of this ethnographic study was to explore how young children learned about literacy in the course of their usual classroom activities. Rowe proposed two research questions that allowed her to take both individual and social perspectives on literacy learning: (1) How are children's understandings and use of written language, music, and graphic/constructive art embedded in the social world of their classroom? (2) How do young children explore the potentials of these communication systems? What social-psychological strategies do they use?

Rowe describes the patterns of intertextual tying made by the twenty-one children as they learned to communicate through writing, art, and music, and presents the theoretical hypotheses she generated to describe the role of intertextuality in the literacy learning process. Rowe suggests that the construction of intertextual connections is a central part of the literacy learning process and argues that there are two general types of intertextual connections that are important in literacy learning. The first type of intertextual connection occurs when children link their

51

existing knowledge about literacy to the demonstrations provided by other authors. The process of mutual intertextualizing
that occurs through conversation and demonstration leads to the
formation of shared meanings about literacy and allows members of the same authoring community to use literacy to communicate with others. The second type of intertextual connection
reflects the mediation of children's existing texts in their literacy
learning. Children interpret their experiences by flexibly linking
their current observations to multiple aspects of their past experiences, creating context-specific hypotheses about literacy.

(*See also* Rowe, D. (1986). *Literacy in the Child's World: Preschoolers' Exploration of Alternate Communication Systems.* Unpublished doctoral dissertation, Indiana University, Bloomington, IN.)

Short, K. (1985). *Literacy as Collaborative Experience.* Unpublished
doctoral dissertation, Indiana University, Bloomington, IN.

Short began her year-long classroom-based study with a dual
focus on collaboration and intertextuality. As she developed curriculum with the teacher and talked about the experience with
the teacher and with her colleagues, she redefined the relationship between her two goals. Rather than perceiving them as
different from one another, she began to view collaboration as
an intertextual process—a means of making meaning from experience. Originally defining text as a written document, she later
redefined it as a "chunk of meaning that we construct from our
world of experience."

In her narrative, Short argues that learners construct texts
(stories) in order to make sense of experience and that storying is
therefore a useful metaphor for learning. She notes that, over the
course of the year, curriculum and research merged as intertextual processes that lead to "practiceable theory."

In addressing intertextuality, Short analyzes the changing
understandings across all participants. She identifies patterns
across all the data to show how the authoring cycle became a
curricular frame and how authorship extended through reading
and writing into all areas of the curriculum. Short argues that
curriculum became an intertextual process and documents the
diversity of intertextual ties, as evidenced by the stories the

children were writing and by the responses they made during interviews.

In her final chapter, Short provides a graphic representation of learning as an intertextual and social process, and uses examples from the data to highlight three perspectives on intertextuality: connecting with past texts, connecting with the texts of others, and connecting with society's texts. Building on Pierce's work on learning, Short takes the stance that learning is a search for unity, and for patterns that connect, for stories, and that it is the tension caused by anomalies, by inconsistencies, that "move the learning process forward . . . to create a new unity or text."

Short suggests that "a learning theory must . . . be a social theory" and that "collaboration is [not] just another variable to consider in learning . . . but [rather] changes the whole nature of the learning process." Aligning herself with Vygotsky's belief that "the social world is already embedded in thought," Short notes that "collaboration changed the nature of our social interactions with each other and . . . this change in social interactions became embedded in the way we thought and learned." Exploring the characteristics of collaboration, she argues that collaboration was "essential to providing the learning environment necessary to facilitate intertextuality and the learning cycle. . . . What the evidence from this study points to is that whenever children or adults are given the opportunity to interact and learn with others, learning is more productive and they are able to think in more complex and divergent ways." Short notes that, "in the past, educational innovators have attempted to hand classroom teachers a solution to their problems . . . but as soon as teachers are left on their own, innovation dies out because they have not been given a way to take ownership of the change process themselves." She suggests that, "as educators, we need to be concerned about developing learning environments that facilitate this learning process. . . . Research has tended to emphasize reflexivity at the expense of action and curriculum in schools has tended to emphasize action at the expense of reflexivity."

(*See also* Harste, J., and Short, K., with Burke, C. (1988). *Creating Classrooms for Authors.* Portsmouth, NH: Heinemann.)

Stephens, D. (1986). *Research and Theory as Practice: A Collaborative Study of Change.* Unpublished doctoral dissertation, Indiana University, Bloomington, IN.

Stephens spent a semester collaborating with Cynthia Brabson in an attempt to integrate reading and writing in Brabson's classroom for intermediate level children labeled learning disabled. The study provides an overview of the collaborative experience, explores the process of curriculum building, and details the progress that students made within an integrated language arts environment.

(*See also* Stephens, D. (1987). Empowering Learning: Research as Practical Theory. *English Education, 19,* 220–228.)

Stice, C., and Bertrand, N. (1989). The Texts and Textures of Literacy Learning in Whole Language Versus Traditional/Skills Classrooms. In S. McCormick and J. Zutell (Eds.), *1989 National Reading Conference Yearbook.*

Stice and Bertrand cite Neisser in arguing that "the two traditional approaches to literacy instruction, i.e. phonics/skills (or the traditional/basal) approach and the decoding, sub-skills (or behavioral/mastery learning) approach have not proved successful in the case of poor minority children." In this study, they examined the effectiveness of whole language instruction for this population. Defining whole language as "a model for literacy instruction which emphasizes a collaborative learning environment for children and focuses on using language as a tool for learning," Stice and Bertrand identified fifty "at-risk" children, "averaging five each in five whole language classrooms, grades one and two, and their matches from traditional/skills classrooms." The students were determined to be "at-risk" if they were "eligible for the school's free lunch program . . . and met three of these four conditions: (1) low achievement as determined by below the mean scores on reading comprehension or total reading sections of the locally administered standardized reading tests, (2) considered at risk of school failure by the classroom teacher, (3) a member of a non-intact nuclear family or (4) living in publicly subsidized housing." They were matched on age, race, sex, and stanine scores on the Stanford Reading Achievement Test.

Reading and writing products were gathered over a two-year period. In addition, Goodman, Watson, and Burke's (1987) Reading Miscue Inventory was used to analyze oral readings audiotaped twice yearly for each child, Clay's Concepts About Print survey was administered in the fall and spring of each year, and students were interviewed about their reading and writing.

Results from the Stanford Achievement Test suggest that "the at-risk children in the emerging whole language classrooms performed as well or better than their matches in the traditional classrooms." On the writing tasks, "the children in the whole language classrooms did as well on traditional spellings as their matches and used more invented spelling." There were no differences on quantitative measures, such as number of words, number of T-units, and number of sentences. Stice and Bertrand note that "the most striking finding, when examining the oral reading miscues and retelling scores for the two types of classrooms is that the retelling scores for the whole language classrooms are consistently and in many instances higher than for the traditional skills classrooms. Whole language children retold longer, more complete versions of their stories." The children in the whole language classroom initially scored lower on Clay's CAP test but scored significantly higher on the posttest. Analyzing interview data, Stice and Bertrand conclude that "children in whole language classrooms had a greater awareness of alternative strategies for dealing with problems . . . appear[ed] to feel better about themselves as readers and writers, focus[ed] more on meaning and the communicative nature of language . . . and, fourth, whole language children appear[ed] to be developing greater independence in both reading and writing. Traditional children seem[ed] to be more dependent on the teacher if their initial strategy fails."

Teale, W., and Martinez, G. (1987). *Connecting Writing: Fostering Emergent Literacy in Kindergarten Children* (Technical Report No. 412). San Antonio, TX: University of Texas at San Antonio.

This report describes how writing was incorporated into a kindergarten emergent literacy program in San Antonio, Texas.

Three types of connections were observed as having a powerful effect on the children's writing development: connecting writing with functional purposes, connecting writing with reading, and connecting children with other children who were experiencing success as writers.

White, J., Vaughan, J., and Rorie, I. L. (1986). Picture of a Classroom Where Reading Is Real. *The Reading Teacher, 36,* 842–845.

This article discusses two first-grade classrooms that provided extensive literacy opportunities for children. In one of these classrooms, the twenty-five children were from lower to lower-middle socioeconomic backgrounds, and all scored above the 54 percent on a standardized reading test administered in the spring of the first grade year. Twenty had grade equivalent scores above 2.0; the other five scored between 1.6 and 1.9. The article uses classroom vignettes and narrative to describe the literacy experiences and successes of the children.

Willert, M., and Kamii, C. (1985). Reading in Kindergarten: Direct Versus Indirect Teaching. *Young Children, 40,* pg. 3–9.

Willert observed her class of six-year-olds in order to identify the strategies they developed as they were learning to read and write. She had taught the children since they were two years old and stressed that she "wanted the children to learn to read eventually but was determined not to give lessons or to impose reading in any other way." At the time of the study, the children were in kindergarten. Willert concluded that "the children appeared to *invent* strategies to figure out or give meaning to written words" and that "the child most advanced in reading appeared to use *many* strategies when reading." She identified six strategies the children devised in learning to read and write:

1. Focusing only on the first letter of the word.
2. Focusing on the configuration of the word, such as length and shape.
3. Getting semantic clues from pictures and situations.
4. Looking for familiar letters and combinations of letters in the rest of the word.

56

5. Practicing spelling and copying words over and over again, until they become known.
6. Inventing and using a phonological system to sound out the words.

Willert and Kamii note that the children made considerable progress as readers and writers but caution that the "issue for educators is not what method produces higher test scores in the early grades. It is what kind of teaching enhances children's *desire* to read, to write well, to acquire more knowledge, to think critically about what they read and to communicate effectively with other people." They suggest that teaching that builds on children's intrinsic interests supports the development of children who can read and who choose to do so.

End Note

In the same year that the Ribowsky study was published, Taylor, Blum, and Logsdon (1986) published a study that compared scores of children in classrooms that it might be possible to consider as "whole language" and "traditional." However, in their study, they refer to these classrooms as "implementing" and "non-implementing" relative to teachers' abilities to make curricular decisions consistent with training provided by the researchers. Because of this ambiguity, their study was not included in this bibliography as a "whole language study." However, I have included a brief abstract of their study so that readers can draw their own conclusions about the "whole language-ness" of the "implementing" classrooms.

Taylor, N., Blum, I., and Logsdon (1986). The Development of Written Language Awareness: Environmental Aspects and Program Characteristics. *Reading Research Quarterly, XXI* (2), 132–149.

Taylor, Blum, and Logsdon trained prekindergarten and kindergarten teachers in what they refer to as "a theory-based pre-reading curriculum." The training began in the summer and continued throughout the year. During this same time period, members of the research team used observational data to identify "essential features of a language- and print-rich curriculum." These features included multiple and varied stimuli for reading, multiple and varied stimuli for writing, accessible and functional display of children's language products, integrative print, classroom routines and child-centered teaching. Based on these features, the research team members assessed classrooms of teachers-in-training to determine whether the "characteristics of the curriculum were (a) implemented very effectively, (b) implemented effectively (c) implemented to a limited degree or (d) not implemented."

They then assessed children from the classrooms, using the Written Language Awareness Test (WLA) and the Boehm Test of Basic Concepts (Boehm). Collapsing the four teacher categories into two—implementing and non-implementing—the researchers compared the scores of the children with the teacher ratings.

The researchers concluded that students in implementing classrooms outperformed students in non-implementing classrooms on the total battery of the WLA and on three of the subtests: the Aural Word Boundaries Test, the Metalinguistic Interview Test and the Rye-Rhinceros Test. They also noted that "differences between groups on the fourth subtest, the Aural Consonent Cloze Task, approached significance." Students from implementing classrooms also outperformed students from non-implementing classrooms on Level I of the Boehm.

The researchers also compared students' scores on the Metropolitan Readiness Test and reported that "students in implementing classrooms outperformed students in non-implementing on two of the three subtests: the visual subtest, which measures letter recognition and visual matching . . . and the language subtest, which measures school language and learning. . . . There were no differences between the groups on the auditory subtest. . . . Group differences on the total battery of MRT tests approached significance. . . ."

Taylor, Blum, and Logsdon (1986) concluded: "Children learn best in a language- and print-rich environment, with many opportunities to observe, try out, and practice literacy skills in genuine communications situations."

References

Aaron, I., Chall, J., Durkin, D., Goodman, K., and Strickland, D. (1990a). Past, Present, and Future of Literacy Education: Comments from a Panel of Distinguished Educators, Part I. *Reading Teacher, 43* (4), 302–311.

———. (1990b). Past, Present, and Future of Literacy Education: Comments from a Panel of Distinguished Educators, Part II. *Reading Teacher, 43* (6), 370–379.

Allen J. (1988). *Literacy Development in Whole Language Kindergartens* (Technical Report No. 436). Urbana-Champaign, IL: University of Illinois, Center for the Study of Reading.

Allen, J., and Carr, E. (1989). Collaborative Learning Among Kindergarten Writers: Jamie Learns How to Read at School. In J. Allen and J. Mason (Eds.), *Risk Makers, Risk Takers, Risk Breakers: Reducing the Risks for Young Literacy Learners.* Portsmouth, NH: Heinemann.

Allen, J., Michalove, B., West, M., and Shockley, B. (1989). *Studying the Students We Worry About: A Collaborative Investigation of Literacy Learning.* Paper presented at the annual meeting of the National Reading Conference, Austin, TX.

Altwerger, B., Edelsky, C., and Flores, B. (1987). Whole Language: What's New? *The Reading Teacher, 41* (2), 144–154.

Anderson, R., Hiebert, E., Scott, J., and Wilkinson, I. (1985). *Becoming a Nation of Readers.* Washington, DC: U.S. Department of Education.

Anderson, R., Spiro, R., and Anderson, T. (1978). Schemata as Scaffolding for the Representations of Information in Connected Discourse. *American Education Research Journal, 15* (3), 433–440.

Apple, M. (1983). Work, Gender and Teaching. *Teachers College Record, 84*, 611–628.

Atwell, N. (1987). *In the Middle.* Portsmouth, NH: Heinemann.

Avery, C. (1985). Lori 'Figures It Out': A Young Writer Learns to Read. In J. Hansen, T. Newkirk, and D. Graves (Eds.), *Breaking Ground: Teachers Relate Reading and Writing in the Elementary School.* Portsmouth, NH: Heinemann.

Baghban, M. (1984). *Our Daughter Learns to Read and Write: A Case Study from Birth to Three.* Newark, DE: International Reading Association.

Baker, L., and Brown, A. (1984). Metacognitive Skills and Reading. In P. D. Pearson (Ed.), *Handbook of Reading Research.* New York: Longman.

Barone, D., and Lovell, J. (1987). Bryan the Brave: A Second Grader's Growth as Reader and Writer. *Language Arts, 64,* 505–515.

Bissex, G. (1980). *GNYS AT WRK: A Child Learns to Write and Read.* Cambridge, MA: Harvard University Press.

———. (1987). *Seeing for Ourselves: Case Study Research by Teachers of Writing.* Portsmouth, NH: Heinemann.

Bloome, D., and Green, J. (1984). Directions in the Sociolinguistic Study of Reading. In P. D. Pearson (Ed.), *Handbook of Reading Research.* New York: Longman.

Boutwell, M. (1983). Reading and Writing: A Reciprocal Agreement. *Language Arts, 60,* 723–730.

Bowerman, M. (1982). Starting to Talk Worse: Clues to Language Acquisition from Children's Late Speech Errors. In S. Strauss (Ed.), *U-Shaped Behavioral Growth.* New York: Academic Press.

Brabson, C. (in process). *The Kinds of Anomalies Encountered While Participating in Literacy Events and the Environmental Conditions That Support Anomalies.* Unpublished doctoral dissertation, Indiana University, Bloomington, IN.

Brown, A. (1980). Metacognitive Development and Reading. In R. J. Spiro, B. C. Bruce, and W. F. Brewer (Eds.), *Theoretical Issues in Reading Comprehension.* Hillsdale, NJ: Erlbaum.

Brown, A., Campione, J., and Day, J. (1981). Learning to Learn: On Training Students to Learn from Texts. *Educational Researcher, 10,* 14–21.

Brown, R. (1970). *Psycholinguistics.* New York: Macmillan.

Burke, C. (1987). Reading Interview. In Y. Goodman, D. Watson, and C. Burke. *Reading Miscue Inventory: Alternative Procedures.* New York: Richard C. Owen.

Carey, S. (1982). Semantic Development: The State of the Art. In W. Gleitman (Ed.), *Language Acquisition: The State of the Art.* Boston: Cambridge University Press.

Church, S., and Newman, J. (1985). Danny: A Case History of an Instructionally Induced Reading Problem. In J. Newman (Ed.), *Whole Language: Theory in Use.* Portsmouth, NH: Heinemann.

Clark, E. V. (1977). Strategies and the Mapping Problem in First Language Acquisition. In J. Macnamara (Ed.), *Language Learning and Thought.* New York: Academic Press.

————. (1978). Strategies for Communicating. *Child Development, 49,* 953–959.

Clarke, M. (1987). Don't Blame the System: Constraints on Whole Language Reform. *Language Arts, 64,* 384–396.

Clay, M. (1972). *Reading: The Patterning of Complex Behavior.* Auckland, New Zealand: Heinemann.

Clyde, J. A. (1987). *A Collaborative Venture: Exploring the Sociopsycholinguistic Nature of Literacy.* Unpublished doctoral dissertation, Indiana University, Bloomington, IN.

Cornbleth, C. (1987). The Persistence of Myth in Teacher Education and Teaching. In T. Popkewitz (Ed.), *Critical Studies in Teacher Education: Its Folklore, Theory and Practice.* London: Falmer Press.

Cousins, P. (1988). *The Social Construction of Learning Problems: Language Use in a Special Education Classroom.* Unpublished doctoral dissertation, Indiana University, Bloomington, IN.

Crowley, P. (in process). *Readers' Views of the Reading Process, Their Own Reading and Reading Curriculum in a Whole Language School* (working title). Unpublished doctoral dissertation, University of Missouri, Columbia, MO.

Dahl, K. (1988). *The Construction of Knowledge About Written Language by Low-SES Learners During Their Kindergarten*

Year. Paper presented at the thirty-seventh annual meeting of the National Reading Conference, Tucson, AZ.

Dahl, K., and Freppon, P. (in process). *An Investigation of the Ways Low-SES Children in Whole Language Classrooms Make Sense of Instruction in Reading and Writing in the Early Grades* (working title).

Dahl, K., and Purcell-Gates, V. (1989). *Patterns of Success at Literacy Learning Among Low-SES Urban Children in the Early Grades.* Paper presented at the thirty-eighth annual meeting of the National Reading Conference, Austin, TX.

DeFord, D. (1981). Literacy: Reading, Writing and Other Essentials. *Language Arts, 6,* 652–658.

DeLawter, J. (1975). The Relationship of Beginning Reading Instruction and Miscue Patterns. In W. Page (Ed.), *Help for the Reading Teacher: New Directions in Research.* Urbana, IL: National Council of Teachers of English.

Delpit, L. (1988). The Silenced Dialogue: Power and Pedagogy in Educating Other People's Children. *Harvard Educational Review, 58* (3), 280–298.

Doake, D. (1985). Reading-Like Behavior: Its Role in Learning to Read. In A. Jaggar and M. T. Smith-Burke (Eds.), *Observing the Language Learner.* Newark, DE: International Reading Association, and Urbana, IL: National Council of Teachers of English.

Dobson, L. (1983). *The Progress of Early Writers as They Discover Written Language for Themselves.* Vancouver, B.C.: Educational Research Institute of British Columbia, Report No. 83:11 (ERIC Document Reproduction Service No. ED 235 505).

———. (1985). Learn to Read by Writing: A Practical Program for Reluctant Readers. *Teaching Exceptional Children, 18,* 30–36.

———. (1988). *Connections in Learning to Write and Read: A Study of Children's Development Through Kindergarten and Grade One* (Technical Report No. 418). Urbana-Champaign, IL: University of Illinois, Center for the Study of Reading.

Durkin, D. (1966). *Children Who Read Early.* New York: Teachers College Press.

———. (1978–1979). What Classroom Observations Reveal About Reading Comprehension Instruction. *Reading Research Quarterly, 14,* 481–533.

Edelsky, C. (1988). Research Currents: Resisting (Professional) Arrest. *Language Arts, 65,* 396–402.

Edelsky, C., Draper, K., and Smith, K. (1983). Hookin 'em in at the Start of School in a Whole Language Classroom. *Anthropology and Education Quarterly, 14,* 257–281.

Edelsky, C., and Smith, K. (1984). Is That Writing—or Are Those Marks Just a Figment of Your Curriculum? *Language Arts, 61,* 24–33.

Everhart, R. (1983). *Reading, Writing, and Resistance: Adolescence and Labor in a Junior High School.* London: Routledge & Kegan Paul.

Ferreiro, E., and Teberosky, A. (1979). *Literacy before Schooling.* Portsmouth, NH: Heinemann.

Five, C. (1985). Teresa: A Reciprocal Learning Experience for Teacher and Child. In J. Harste and D. Stephens (Eds.), *Toward Practical Theory.* Bloomington, IN: Indiana University, Language Education Department.

Flavell, J. (1976). Metacognitive Aspects of Problem-Solving. In L. B. Resnick (Ed.), *The Nature of Intelligence.* Hillsdale, NJ: Erlbaum.

Florio-Ruane, S. (1986). *Conversation and Narrative in Collaborative Research* (Occasional Paper No. 102). East Lansing, MI: Michigan State University, Institute for Research on Teaching.

Fraatz, J. M. (1987). *The Politics of Reading.* New York: Teachers College Press.

Freppon, P. (1988). *An Investigation of Children's Concepts of the Purpose and Nature of Reading Indifferent Instructional Settings.* Unpublished doctoral dissertation, University of Cincinnati, Cincinnati, OH.

García, G. E., Jiménez, R., and Pearson, P. D. (1989). *Annotated Bibliography of Research Related to the Reading of At-Risk Children* (Technical Report No. 482). Urbana-Champaign, IL: University of Illinois, Center for the Study of Reading.

García, G., Stephens, D., Koenke, K., Pearson, D., Harris, V., and Jiménez, R. (1989). *A Study of Classroom Practices Related to the Reading of Low-Achieving Students: Phase One* (Study 2.2.3.5). Urbana-Champaign, IL: University of Illinois, Center for the Study of Reading.

Giroux, H. (1984). Rethinking the Language of Schooling. *Language Arts, 61,* 33–40.

Goodman, K. (1973). *The Psycholinguistic Nature of the Reading Process.* Detroit, MI: Wayne State University Press.

———. (1984). Becoming Readers in a Complex Society. *National Society for the Study of Education, Eighty-Third Yearbook.* Chicago, IL: University of Chicago Press.

———. (1986). What's Whole in Whole Language? Portsmouth, NH: Heinemann.

Goodman, Y. (1989). Roots of the Whole Language Movement. *Elementary School Journal, 90* (2), 113–127.

Goodman, Y., and Burke, C. (1972). *Reading Miscue Inventory Complete Kit: Procedure for Diagnosis and Evaluation.* New York: Macmillan.

Goodman, Y., Watson, D., and Burke, C. (1987). *Reading Miscue Inventory: Alternative Procedures.* New York: Richard C. Owen.

Graves, D. (1983). *Writing: Teachers and Children at Work.* Portsmouth, NH: Heinemann.

Gunderson, L., and Shapiro, J. (1987). Some Findings on Whole Language Instruction. *Reading Canada Lecture, 5,* 22–26.

———. (1988). Whole Language Instruction: Writing in First Grade. *Reading Teacher, 41,* 430–439.

Hagerty, P., Hiebert, E., and Owens, M. K. (1989). Students' Comprehension, Writing and Perceptions in Two Approaches to Literacy Instruction. In S. McCormick and J. Zutell (Eds.), *1989 National Reading Conference Yearbook.*

Halliday, M. (1978). *Language as Social Semiotic.* Baltimore, MD: University Park Press.

———. (1975). *Learning How to Mean: Explorations in the Function of Language.* London: Edward Arnold.

———. (1982). Three Aspects of Children's Language Development: Learning Language, Learning Through Language, Learning About Language. In Y. Goodman, M. Haussler, and D. Strickland (Eds.), *Oral and Written Language Development Research: Impact on the Schools.* Urbana, IL: National Council of Teachers of English.

Hansen, J. (1987). *When Writers Read.* Portsmouth, NH: Heinemann.

Hansen, J., Newkirk, T., and Graves, D. (1985). *Breaking Ground: Teachers Relate Reading and Writing in the Elementary School.* Portsmouth, NH: Heinemann.

Hanssen, E. (in process). *The Social Creation of Meaning: Learning as a Dialogic Process.* Unpublished doctoral dissertation, Indiana University, Bloomington, IN.

Harste, J., and Short, K., with Burke, C. (1988). *Creating Classrooms for Authors.* Portsmouth, NH: Heinemann.

Harste, J., and Stephens, D. (Eds.). (1985). *Toward Practical Theory: A State of Practice Assessment of Reading Comprehension Instruction* (Final report USDE-C-300-83-0130). Bloomington, IN: Indiana University, Language Education Department.

Harste, J., Woodward, V., and Burke, C. (1984). *Language Stories and Literacy Lessons.* Portsmouth, NH: Heinemann.

Haussler, M. (1982). *Transitions into Literacy: A Psycholinguistic Analysis of Beginning Reading in Kindergarten and First Grade Children.* Unpublished doctoral dissertation, University of Arizona, Tucson, AZ.

Heap, J. (1989). *Reading as Rational Action: Functioning and Literacy in Daily Life.* Paper presented at National Reading Conference, Tucson, AZ.

Heath, S. B. (1983). *Ways with Words: Language, Life, and Work in Communities and Classrooms.* Cambridge, England: Cambridge University Press.

Holdaway, D. (1986). The Structure of Natural Learning as a Basis for Literacy Instruction. In M. Sampson (Ed.), *The Pursuit of Literacy: Early Reading and Writing.* Dubuque, IA: Kendall/Hunt.

————. (1979). *The Foundations of Literacy.* Sidney, Australia: Ashton Scholastic Book Services.

Jaggar, A., and Smith-Burke, T. (Eds.). (1985). *Observing the Language Learner.* Newark, DE: International Reading Association, and Urbana, IL: National Council of Teachers of English.

Johnson, D. W., and Johnson, R. T. (1979). Conflict in the Classroom: Controversy and Learning. *Review of Educational Research, 49,* 51–70.

Johnston, P., and Allington, R. (in press). Remediation. In P. D. Pearson (Ed.), *Handbook of Reading Research* (Vol. 2). New York: Longman.

Kirsch, I. S., and Jungeblut, A. (1986). *Literacy: Profiles of America's Young Adults.* Princeton, NJ: NAEP & ETS.

Lindfors, J. (1980). *Children's Language and Learning.* Englewood Cliffs, NJ: Prentice-Hall.

————. (1985). Understanding the Development of Language Structure. In A. Jaggar and T. Smith-Burke (Eds.), *Observing the Language Learner.* Newark, DE: International Reading Association, and Urbana, IL: National Council of Teachers of English.

McConaghy, J. (1986). *Literature, Literacy and Young Children.* Unpublished master's thesis, University of Alberta, Edmonton, Canada.

Mervar, K., and Hiebert, E. (1989). Literature Selection Strategies and Amount of Reading in Two Literacy Approaches. In S. McCormick and J. Zutell (Eds.), *1989 National Reading Conference Yearbook.*

Michalove, B. (1989). *Engagement and Community in a Second Grade Classroom.* Paper presented at the annual meeting of the National Reading Conference, Austin, TX.

Mills, H. (1986). *Writing Evaluation: A Transactional Process.* Unpublished doctoral dissertation, Indiana University, Bloomington, IN.

Mills, H., and Clyde, J. A. (1990). *Portraits of Whole Language Classrooms.* Portsmouth, NH: Heinemann.

Munsch, R. (1989). *Love You Forever.* Ontario, Canada: Firefly Books.

Neilsen, A. R. (1989). *Critical Thinking and Reading: Empowering Learners to Think and Act.* Urbana, IL: National Council of Teachers of English.

Neisser, U. (1976). *Cognition and Reality.* San Francisco: W. H. Freeman.

Newkirk, T., and Atwell, N. (1985). *Breaking Ground: Teachers Relate Reading and Writing in the Elementary School.* Portsmouth, NH: Heinemann.

Newman, J. (1984). *The Craft of Children's Writing.* Ontario, Canada: Scholastic-TAB publications.

———. (1985). *Whole Language: Theory in Use.* Portsmouth, NH: Heinemann.

———. (1990). *Finding Our Own Way.* Portsmouth, NH: Heinemann.

Newman, J., and Church, S. (1990). Myths of Whole Language. *Reading Teacher,* 44 (1), 20–26.

Ogbu, J. (1986). The Consequences of the American Caste System. In U. Neisser (Ed.), *The School Achievement of Minority Children: New Perspective.* Hillsdale, NJ: Erlbaum, 19–56.

Pearson, P. D., Hansen, J., and Gordon, C. (1979). The Effective Background Knowledge on Young Children's Comprehension of Explicit and Implicit Information. *Journal of Reading Behavior,* 11, 201–209.

Pearson, P. D., and Stephens, D. (in process). *The Relationship Between Assessment and Instruction* (working title).

Pierce, V. (1984). *Bridging the Gap Between Language Research/ Theory and Practice: A Case Study.* Unpublished doctoral dissertation, Texas Woman's University, Denton, TX.

Popkewitz, T. (1987). *Critical Studies in Teacher Education: Its Folklore, Theory and Practice.* London, England: The Falmer Press.

Purcell-Gates, V. (1988). Lexical and Syntactic Knowledge of Written Narrative Held by Well-Read-To Kindergarten and Second Graders. *Research in the Teaching of English, 22,* 128–160.

Routman, R. (1988). *Transitions.* Portsmouth, NH: Heinemann.

Read, C. (1975). Lessons to Be Learned from the Preschool Orthographer. In E. H. Lennenberg and E. Lennenberg (Eds.), *Foundations of Language Development: A Multidisciplinary Approach* (Vol. 2). New York: Academic Press.

Rhodes, L., and Shanklin, N. (1990). *A Research Base for Whole Language.* Denver, CO: LINK.

Rhodes, L., and Shannon, J. (1982). Psycholinguistic Principles in Operation in a Primary Learning Disabilities Classroom. *Topics in Learning and Learning Disabilities, 1–10.*

Ribowsky, H. (1986). *The Comparative Effects of a Code Emphasis Approach and a Whole Language Approach upon Emergent Literacy of Kindergarten Children.* Unpublished doctoral dissertation, New York University, New York, NY.

Rigg, P., and Enright, D. S. (1986). *Children and ESL: Integrating Perspectives.* Washington, DC: Teachers of English to Speakers of Other Languages.

Rowe, D. W. (1986). *Literacy in the Child's World: Preschoolers' Exploration of Alternate Communication Systems.* Unpublished doctoral dissertation, Indiana University, Bloomington, IN.

———. (1987). Literacy Learning as an Intertextual Process. In J. Readance and R. S. Baldwin (Eds.), *Research in Literacy: Merging Perspectives.* Thirty-Sixth Yearbook of the National Reading Conference. Rochester, NY: National Reading Conference.

Rumelhart, D. and Ortony, A. (1977). The Representation of Knowledge in Memory. In R. C. Anderson, R. J. Spiro, and W. E. Montague (Eds.), *Schooling and the Acquisition of Knowledge*. Hillsdale, NJ: Erlbaum.

Sampson, M. (Ed.). (1986). *The Pursuit of Literacy: Early Reading and Writing*. Dubuque, IA: Kendall/Hunt.

Schon, D. (1983). *The Reflective Practitioner*. NY: Basic Books.

Shannon, P. (1989a). *Broken Promises*. Granky, MA: Bergin & Garvey.

———. (1989b). The Struggle for Control of Literacy Lessons. *Language Arts, 66*, 625–634.

Shockley, B. (1989). *Sing a Song of Joseph*. Paper presented at the annual meeting of the National Reading Conference, Austin, TX.

Short, K. (1985). *Literacy as Collaborative Experience*. Unpublished doctoral dissertation, Indiana University, Bloomington, IN.

Siegel, M., and Carey, R. F. (1989). *Critical Thinking: A Semiotic Perspective*. Urbana, IL: National Council of Teachers of English.

Simon, R. (1987). Empowerment as a Pedagogy of Possibility. *Language Arts, 64*, 384–401.

Slavin, R. E. (1983). *Cooperative Learning*. New York: Longman.

Smith, N. B. (1934). *American Reading Instruction*. NY: Silver, Burdett.

Stanovich, K. (1986). Matthew Effects in Reading: Some Consequences of Individual Differences in the Acquisition of Literacy. *Reading Research Quarterly, 21*, 360–407.

Stephens, D. (1986). *Research and Theory as Practice: A Collaborative Study of Change*. Unpublished doctoral dissertation, Indiana University, Bloomington, IN.

———. (1987). Empowering Learning: Research as Practical Theory. *English Education, 19*, 220–228.

———. (1988). *Collaborative Research as Methodological Choice.* Paper presented at American Educational Research Association, New Orleans, LA.

———. (1990). *What Matters: A Primer for Teaching Reading.* Portsmouth, NH: Heinemann.

Stephens, D., and Harste, J. (1985). Accessing the Potential of the Learner: Towards an Understanding of the Complexities of Context. *Peabody Journal of Education, 62,* 86–99.

Stephens, D., Pearson, P. D., Stallman, A., Commeyras, M., Shelton, J., Weinzierl, J., Rodriquez, A., and Roe, M. (1990). Assessment and Decision Making in the Schools: Four Case Studies (Study 2.4.1.1b). Urbana-Champaign, IL: University of Illinois, Center for the Study of Reading.

Stice, C. (in process). *Routes to Whole Language: An Annotated Bibliography of Research and Theory from Which Whole Language Is Derived.*

Stice, C., and Bertrand, N. (in press). The Texts and Textures of Literacy Learning in Whole Language versus Traditional/ Skills Classrooms. In S. McCormick and J. Zutell (Eds.), *1989 National Reading Conference Yearbook.*

Story, J. (1988). Personal communication.

Story, J., and Stephens, D. (in process). *"You Should Have Known": Tales of a Very Hard Year* (working title).

Sulzby, E., and Teale, W. (1987). *Young Children's Storybook Reading: Longitudinal Study of Parent-Child Interaction and Children's Independent Functioning.* Ann Arbor, MI: University of Michigan.

Taylor, D. (1983). *Family Literacy.* Portsmouth, NH: Heinemann.

Taylor, N., Blum, I., and Logsdon, D. (1986). The Development of Written Language Awareness: Environmental Aspects and Program Characteristics. *Reading Research Quarterly, XXI* (2), 132–149.

Teale, W., and Martinez, G. (1987). *Connecting Writing: Fostering Emergent Literacy in Kindergarten Children* (Technical Report

No. 412). San Antonio, TX: University of Texas at San Antonio.

Vygotsky, L. S. (1962). *Thought and Language.* Cambridge, MA: MIT Press.

Wanner, E., and Gleitman, L. R. (1982). *Language Acquisition: The State of the Art.* Cambridge, MA: Cambridge University Press.

Watson, D., Burke, C., and Harste, J. (1988). *Whole Language: Inquiring Voices.* Ontario, Canada: Scholastic-TAB.

Weaver, C. (1990). Weighing Claims of "Phonics First" Advocates. *Education Week,* March, 23, 32.

Wells, G. (1986). *The Meaning Makers.* Portsmouth, NH: Heinemann.

Wendler, D., Samuels, S. J., and Moore, U. K. (1989). The Comprehension Instruction of Award Winning Teachers, Teachers with Master's Degrees, and Other Teachers. *Reading Research Quarterly, 24,* 382–401.

White, J., Vaughan, J., and Rorie, I. L. (1986). Picture of a Classroom Where Reading Is Real. *Reading Teacher, 36,* 842–845.

Whitin, D., Mills., H., and O'Keefe, T. (in press). *Living and Learning Mathematics: Stories and Strategies for Supporting Mathematical Literacy.* Portsmouth, NH: Heinemann.

Willert, M., and Kamii, C. (1985). Reading in Kindergarten: Direct Versus Indirect Teaching. *Young Children, 40,* 3–9.

About the Author

Diane Stephens is currently an Assistant Professor at the University of Illinois at Urbana-Champaign. She teaches language and literacy courses for the College of Education and conducts field based research for the Center for the Study of Reading. She brings to that current work her experience as an Assistant Professor at the University of North Carolina as a Reading Resource and High School Equivalency Instructor in public schools, and an Assistant Clinical Supervisor at the Learning Development Center, Rochester Institute of Technology. She has presented at IRA, NRC, and NCTE, among other conferences, and has conducted field research for nearly ten years. She received her doctorate from Indiana University at Bloomington in 1986. She considers herself a teacher researcher who conducts literacy research in her own classroom as well as in the classrooms of others.